I0105784

ANNOYING THINGS MEN NEED TO LEARN

How to Flush the Toilet, Fold Laundry, Replace the Toilet Paper Roll, Listen, Clean Up, Take Out the Trash, and More!

Megan Burke

Copyright 2024.

SPOTLIGHT MEDIA

ISBN: 978-1-951806-61-3

For questions, please reach out to:

Support@ActivityWizo.com

All Rights Reserved.

No part of this book may be reproduced or transmitted in any form or by any means, electronic or mechanical, including photocopying, recording, or by any other form without written permission from the publisher.

FREE BONUS

SCAN TO GET OUR NEXT
BOOK FOR FREE!

Table of Contents

INTRODUCTION

This book was not designed to make fun of the men of the home; just a fun look at some of the silly things that can really add up. We love our men and want them to just change one or two (okay, maybe twenty) things to make the household run a little more smoothly. Men, if you are guilty of any of these faux pas, then look through this book and see what solutions you can pursue to live a happier, more harmonious lifestyle with your spouse.

No matter how much the women in your life love you, there are some common things men do that drives them up a wall. Whether failing to separate the colors from the whites while doing laundry, or leaving the seat up every time they use the bathroom during the night (and women all know how much fun that is to find out the hard way, especially in the middle of the night!), However small they seem, these little problems tend to add up over time.

Unfortunately, when a woman has a man in her life who doesn't seem to understand how frustrating these little things can be, it can drive her crazy. This guidebook is designed to help you understand the small nuances and pet peeves that most women experience. Sure, these habits may not seem like a big deal all on their own, but when added together and explored more in-depth, it is no wonder that women often wonder about living on their own.

Inside this guidebook, we are going to take a light-hearted look at some of the little things that men tend to do without thinking about it. While you may not do all of them, you likely have made some of these faux pas that make the woman in your life pull out their hair or consider an impulsive move to Peru.

But it is not all bad news, fellas! While we may point out key areas for improvement, we'll also provide simple and practical advice that helps you fix any problems and bring harmony back into your life and relationship. It really is the simple things in life that make all the difference, and with this guidebook, you can find the exact activities that you do that tend to drive her up a wall. So, let's dive in and learn those bad habits that tend to drive women crazy.

CHAPTER ONE:
TOILET TIDBITS

The bathroom seems like such a simple spot in the home. A place to relieve yourself, get cleaned up, and prepare for the day. But it is amazing how differently men and women utilize this very important room in the home.

LEAVING THE SEAT UP

Leaving the toilet seat up is something that many women complain about with their partners. But why is it such a big deal? It can be easy to neglect such a small action when you are in a rush, but it only takes a few seconds to put the seat back down.

Most women have a story about going to the bathroom and not paying full attention – whether it's because it's in the middle of the night or they are dealing with the kids – they go to sit down and end up shockingly surprised when they fall in! Now, they're covered in toilet water and either rudely awakened from a half sleep or having to add it to the list of stressors preoccupying their minds. It is unpleasant, uncomfortable, and not that much fun.

As a man, take that few seconds longer to set the seat back down. It doesn't slow you down that much and can be a great way to prevent a partner from becoming unhappy. If you tend to forget, they make stickers for the inside of the toilet lid with silly sayings reminding you to put the seat back down. There are also comical bathroom plaques as well that can help you show courtesy to the women in the house.

FORGETTING TO REPLACE THE TOILET ROLL

It is the argument that is as old as time: Who used the last of the toilet paper? Although it's not always the case, usually it's the man of the house who has delegated the important task of replacing the toilet paper roll. This can lead to an all-out war when the woman needs to use the restroom, but there is no toilet paper in sight.

Guys, replacing the toilet paper roll can make your life so much easier! Take an extra 30 seconds when you are done using the bathroom and grab another roll. Don't just set it on the back of the toilet either. This will cause others in the house to scramble around, looking for it and wondering where the roll went. Instead, place it back in its proper spot and make your partner happy!

Note: Make sure to ask whether the roll should go under or over. This is another hot topic in many relationships, and it is important to get it right from the beginning!

"DECORATING" THE RIM

No one wants to walk into the bathroom and see a mess left behind. It may not seem like a big deal to see a few drops on the toilet seat, but when you have to take extra time to clean it up before you can go, you may be singing a different tune.

Your partner is not your mother. She does not want to clean up after you. Honestly, to have a grown adult living in the house who still needs someone to clean up after them should be a little embarrassing. If you have children or pets, chances are the woman in your life is already doing a lot of invisible labor cleaning up after the household.

In general, unless you are an infant, it's your responsibility to save others from having to encounter your unwanted bodily substances, whether it's a dirty tissue on the floor, beard shavings in the sink, or urine on the toilet seat. The good news is that the steps are simple to get it all cleaned up.

To avoid unnecessary conflict, get in the habit of checking the perimeter before you leave. It only takes a minute to wipe off any stray drops to prevent the woman in your life (or an unlucky guest) from having to deal with it for you.

NEGLECTING
TO FLUSH

Leaving stuff behind in the toilet is not only rude, but it can make the whole bathroom stink. While it's normal to be in a hurry and occasionally forget all about flushing, it is not kind to the other people in the home. This is even more true if you end up leaving, and no one comes home for a long time.

As an adult, you can keep a checklist of everything that needs to get done when you are in the bathroom. You are not a kid who is likely to forget. Some may even assume that you were not forgetful or in a hurry, but that you left the mess behind on purpose. This will not reflect kindly on you with others in your home.

Find some method to help you remember to flush the toilet when you are done. Make a checklist, sing a song, or take a few extra seconds so you don't feel rushed when you need to go. This will help make sure you are prepared and can flush the toilet without leaving anything behind for someone else to deal with.

MISSING THE TRASH CAN

So, you did a great job taking the roll off the dispenser and you even took the time to replace it. You are winning brownie points all over the place and showing off what an outstanding guy you are. But then it comes time to throw away the empty roll of toilet paper, and you miss!

Don't miss the trash can when it's time to throw away those empty rolls of toilet paper — it's not far away. Sure, you can take a few seconds and pretend you are an NBA basketball player attempting to make that crazy shot each time. But if you miss, take the time to pick up the roll.

If you decide not to pick up the empty roll, it just sits there until someone else comes in, and now they have to spend extra time cleaning up. This goes for any bathroom trash. Even one item can stick out like a sore thumb if the woman in your life has invested the time and effort to keep everything clean.

TAKING AN ETERNITY IN THERE

Are you taking a business call and about to make a million dollars on a big merger? Are you writing the next great American novel? Are you catching up on a month's worth of emails?

You partner isn't sure what you are doing in there, and this can be frustrating, especially if you have only one bathroom that everyone needs to share. You can spend an hour or more in there, while everyone else in the home suffers and doesn't get any time before running off to work or school.

Even worse, you get to enjoy a mini vacation in the bathroom, while your partner is about ready to jump off a cliff because the kids are going crazy. Your partner knows you aren't oblivious to the noise outside the door; the neighbors have even come over and are concerned.

You ask yourself, "Maybe it's time to get an alarm or a timer?" If you are the guy who does this in the house, put a timer on yourself and realize you don't need all that time to finish your business. Hurry it up and get out of the bathroom as quickly as possible.

With this in mind, there is nothing wrong with taking a few moments to yourself. Just keep in mind, others might be waiting as patiently as they can. If you want bonus points, create the same space for your lady to take her time in there too when it's her turn. If you have littles in the house, she most likely doesn't even get to go in there alone most of the time. The gesture will go a long way.

IGNORING THE "COURTESY FLUSH"

The courtesy flush, which refers to when you flush while sitting on the toilet, will make the bathroom more enjoyable for everyone who walks in the door. The longer it sits there, the more it will stink up the bathroom and make it unpleasant for others to come into the room.

Of course, most people assume that you wait until you are all done with the toilet before you flush it. When you are done with your business in the bathroom, you can whisk it all away at the same time. But the smell can stick around for longer than you would like. When you do the courtesy flush, it can remove everything before the smell gives you away.

Sure, flushing the toilet and not leaving anything behind is always important. It allows you to take care of business and leave the bathroom looking clean. But, if your business is messy and someone else will use the bathroom when you are done, it is always a good idea to do a courtesy flush to avoid issues and show some care for the other people in the area.

CHAPTER TWO:
THE LAUNDRY
LABYRINTHS

The laundry room seems to be the one room in the home that men fear. They hardly ever go in there, unless they are looking for socks, and seem to magically think that someone should place all the clothing items back in the dresser for them. However, it's not a woman's job to do everyone's laundry, and being an adult means knowing how to do your own laundry. Let's look at some of the major problems men seem to have inside the laundry room.

MIXING COLORS AND WHITES

There is a right way to do the laundry, and then there is a wrong way, such as mixing colors and whites. While it may not matter as much for some clothing, for others, the colors can bleed and ruin some of the best clothing you own.

One rogue red sock is enough to ruin the whole load of white shirts, socks, and blankets that are added to the laundry; no one wants to run around wearing a pink shirt that should be white. This will make everyone in the home upset, so learn how to separate out the colors.

The first goal should be to make sure that anything white is separated from all the colors. Whites should go in their own load, with some safe bleach to help bring out the shine and make them last longer. From there, you can also sort out the light-colored clothing from the dark clothing. Dark clothing, especially black clothes, tend to bleed dye when they are washed. This can stain or darken lighter colored clothes.

Even if you never did laundry at home, you can tell the difference between white and every other color in the rainbow. Take the time to sort out the colors of your next load of laundry to help your clothes last longer and maintain their vibrancy!

THE MYSTERY OF THE DISAPPEARING SOCKS

Where do all the socks go? You put all the pairs into the washer together, but by the time you pull them out, some are missing! This is a big problem that can happen in many households, and the longer you live there, the more socks that seem to disappear. But for some reason, it seems like men lose more of their socks than anyone else in the home.

So, where do they go? The main assumption is that the men are not placing all their socks into the laundry at the same time. They may take the socks off and throw them all around the room, not paying much attention to where they land. When they go to pick the socks up, it is likely that a few will be left behind.

Notice that horrible stink in the bathroom or that lost sock left in the car? These are the disappearing socks. But by the time they are found, the socks are so disgusting that it is likely they end up in the trash.

Men need to step up and find a good solution to this problem. Rather than throwing your socks all over the place, take the time to place both socks in the hamper the moment you take them off.

It is that simple! Sure, it takes a few seconds longer than just throwing them around, but the amount of money you will save on new socks— not to mention the saved looks of exasperation when another stinky one is found—will be worth it.

USING EVERY ITEM
AS AN EXCUSE
NOT TO IRON

Let's just let the cat out of the bag right now; no one likes ironing. Your partner does not like doing it, other men do not like doing it, and even your parents and grandparents were not fans of it. Ironing is not only time-consuming, but it's so easy to mess up and do improperly. Finding a way to avoid ironing on occasion is not a big deal, but when you decide to wear every item in the closet instead of ironing, it can get annoying.

Keep in mind that your partner does not enjoy ironing more than you do. They do not want to take care of all your nice shirts and pants to get you prepared for work. However, if you decide to wear the wrong outfit to work or church enough times, they may feel obligated to do the ironing just so you have something nice to wear.

Take the time to get the ironing done. You can choose whether to do it all at once when the laundry is done, or you may do each individual item as you need it. Stop leaving those wrinkled outfits sitting out and expecting someone else to take on the task of ironing for you.

SHRINKING FAVORITE CLOTHES

The woman in your life has a favorite shirt or other item of clothing that they want to wear all the time. They love the way it looks and feels on them and showing it off is one of the highlights of their day. But then the worst thing happens. You decide to "help" out, all of a sudden, and the favorite outfit has shrunk to half its size and there is no way to save the damage.

Men, it is time to learn how to properly handle the different items of clothing and how to take care of them. Washing clothes improperly is not only a childish move, but can also ruin a favorite shirt, pants, dress, or other piece.

Preferably, you will learn how to properly wash the said item if you want to help. Worst case, if you have no idea how to clean a piece of clothing, then set it to the side and ask. Don't lump that special item together with all the rest and then cause tears at the end of laundry time.

OVERLOADING THE WASHING MACHINE

The washing machine is your best friend. It keeps all your clothes clean and fresh, no matter how hard the kids play outside or what type of work their parents do. Keeping the washing machine in good working order and knowing how to use it properly will not only make a world of difference, but it will also speed up drying time.

Problems arise when men decide to overload the washing machine. This plan may seem logical at first glance—add more clothes into each load and get the work done faster. But this strategy is not as great as it seems, as you run the risk of the clothes not getting completely clean due to the machine being packed too full. The washing machine can get off-kilter and stop working, make loud sounds, or take twice as long for the dryer to do its job.

Men, if you are trying to help your partner, learn how to load up the washing machine the correct way. Overloading it and adding too many clothes to the machine at the same time can at best slow down the process and at worst break your machine.

NEVER EMPTYING
THE POCKETS

For any woman who has had to do her partner's laundry, pockets can be a common trap. While men are big enough to fill those pockets with everything under the sun, they tend to never outgrow the boyish habit of leaving items in them.

This leaves the person doing the laundry with one of two choices. They either ignore all the items that are in the pockets—and face the consequences—or take the extra time to check every pocket before washing. Laundry is a big enough chore, so why leave them with this extra work to do each day?

If your loved one takes the time to empty the pockets, this is extra work. They must search through two to four pockets, sometimes more, in every pair of paints, coat, and anything else that may have a pocket. This can take some time and slow down the whole laundry process. It's irritating to find all that trash (not to mention valuables like cash or keys) in your man's pockets, all the while knowing that he can't be bothered to clean out his own clothes.

The alternative is even worse. Maybe you have decided you are in a hurry and throw all the clothes in the washer, without checking the pockets. Inevitably, this will happen the one time something important is put into the wash and ruined, such as an important paper that is needed, a driver's license or credit card, or something else that is now mush. Even when the offending object is something as trivial as a stray tissue, this is enough to ruin the whole load, as it will get torn up and tossed around the machine in a million little pieces.

Neither of these scenarios is ideal, but it really isn't the responsibility of the women of the home to take care of what is in someone else's pockets. Take a few minutes at the end of the day to empty the pockets and make sure nothing is inside. It doesn't take long to do, but in the end, it can save a lot of rolled eyes and frustration from others in the home.

CHAPTER THREE: COMMUNICATION CONUNDRUMS

Communication is key in any relationship, but due to the different cultural expectations, many men seem to struggle with it. A simple message can get lost in translation and while they may try to blame the woman for some of this, often it falls on the shoulders of forgetful men who choose to pay more attention to their devices. Some of the biggest communication conundrums many men run into include:

THE "FINE"
TRANSLATION MANUAL

The word "fine" can be a loaded bomb. Sometimes, women mean it when they say they are fine. However, other times, she isn't really "fine." Discernment in these cases can go a long way!

Many men don't pay attention to these nuances and miss out on the opportunity to learn how to read the room and communicate. Yes, this does require some listening and focusing, but taking the extra time to pay attention to subtle cues can make a world of difference.

It's important to remember that sometimes, women really are fine when they say they are fine – it's not a loaded response. If you automatically assume there is a problem, it could inadvertently create one. Instead of jumping to conclusions, take the time to ask thoughtful questions about her day or her feelings.

If she isn't feeling fine and wants to talk, then asking a few questions will give her a safe place to talk about what's on her mind without an argument. Paying attention to their tone of voice and body language can help tremendously with giving you clues on whether there is more to the tricky answer "fine." If you love the other person, whether it is a friend or a partner, then take the time to discover the true meaning behind the answer.

REMEMBERING ANNIVERSARIES

How hard is it to remember an important anniversary? Men often can remember a million stats about their favorite football team. They can remember that one event in high school that happened 30 years ago. They can even remember the day that they brought the family dog home. But for some reason, remembering an important anniversary can seem almost impossible.

Men, there is nothing worse than forgetting an anniversary, especially a big one like your wedding date. Yes, life will get busy, and it can be easy to forget what day of the week it is. When you add in kids, school, work, and all the other obligations, you may not even realize it when an important date rolls around. It is time to step up and make a difference; this year, you will remember the anniversary.

Setting reminders in your phone or calendar a few days in advance is always a good call. The earlier you set your reminders, the easier it will be to plan a gift or outing to remind the woman in your life how important they are to you. From calendar apps, reminder notifications, and help from friends and others, there isn't a good reason to forget an important date. So, find the method that works for you and use it!

DECIPHERING THE "DO I LOOK FAT IN THIS?" ENIGMA

This is the dreaded question. No guy likes to be caught on the receiving end of it. It may seem like such a basic question, one where you say "yes" or "no." However, telling someone they look fat or bad in an outfit can land you in some hot water.

First off, never tell a woman that she looks fat. You are the main person in her life, the one she has chosen to spend time with, and the one whose opinion she values most. If you think she is fat, it can cause her whole self-confidence to go down the drain.

Of course, you don't want to lie to your partner about an outfit that doesn't look that great. Yes, you want your wife or partner to feel good in what they wear, but if the outfit is fitting them wrong, or the color looks wrong, lying about it can also get you into some hot water later as well.

Also, just because an outfit doesn't accentuate or flatter a woman's body, doesn't mean she looks fat—sometimes a particular clothing choice simply doesn't work. There are many ways to convey that she would look better in a different outfit, without being cruel or ruining her whole evening.

If your partner asks this question and you think they look amazing in the outfit, then let them know. Pile on the praise and make them feel like the beautiful queen they are. They deserve your love and attention, and praise can help them feel good and prove you genuinely mean it.

Now, if the outfit is not the best on them, this doesn't mean that you must be unkind. You can be honest without being cruel. Don't tell her she looks fat or bad in the outfit. Instead, suggest another outfit that she may look nicer in. For example, you can say something like:

- "That outfit isn't bad, but what about that black dress you haven't worn in a while?"
- "I like that outfit, but where we are going is a little more formal. What are some other options that may look nice and let you dress up more?"

You can even suggest a few accessories that can help the outfit look a bit better as well, such as a sweater or jacket, belt, or even the right pair of shoes. This approach will help your partner look and feel their very best, without feeling let down if you don't like the outfit. Finally, keep in mind that you may not always be expected to have the fashion sense or critical eye to contribute to the conversation. The biggest point to remember is that your partner is asking for your opinion because they don't want to go out looking the best they can. They are seeking your input because your opinion matters to them.

PRETENDING TO LISTEN WHILE ON DEVICES

No one likes to talk to their partner and feel ignored. Your partner most likely gives you undivided attention frequently, listening to you complain about work, learning some of your favorite games, and paying attention to subjects they have no background knowledge about. If they can sit through this while being bored out of their minds, you can return the favor.

Your partner has probably gotten mad at you along the way when you pretend to listen, but you are really paying attention to your device. When we talk about devices, we mean the phone, the computer, or even the gaming system.

You may try assuring her that you are listening, but when you are defeating the villain or trying to get to the next level, is your attention really on her or the game? When checking your emails or text messages, how much are you really absorbing from the other person talking right next to you?

You aren't as good at listening while on your device as you think you are. This may be disappointing news, but it is the truth. Honestly, women can tell when you have more of your focus on the gaming system or phone than on them, which can result in frustration and anger. It's a solid practice to pause your game or put your phone face down while your partner is talking to you. Giving them your full attention is the easiest way to avoid her feeling neglected or unseen.

OVERUSING "I DON'T KNOW" AND "WHATEVER"

These two terms are some of the worst in the English language. They take all the responsibility off you and place it on the other person. In many cases, "whatever" can be rude and insulting as well.

It is fine to say "I don't know" to a question if you honestly don't know something. However, this is used more as a cop-out rather than a true answer. If your partner is asking you to look up something for them or whether you know certain details someone else shared with you, then be present and help them out. Don't say "I don't know" and then expect them to figure it all out.

During an argument, don't fall back on the trusty "whatever" and hope it is going to work out. This sounds insulting and like you don't really care what the other person has said or is feeling at the time. You likely already know this, but using that term helps you stay in control and forces the responsibility back on your partner. It is not only passive aggressive, but it shuts down communication and likely doesn't help you get what you want either.

Communication is key to any relationship; you need to take the time to talk with your partner as much as possible. When you use terms and phrases like the ones above, you close the door on communication and make it hard for anyone to talk with you at all. If you really are uncertain about something, you can still contribute to the conversation by offering a solution. Saying something like, "I'm not sure, but I can look it up" or "I don't know, but I can ask them tomorrow" can go a long way. If you are feeling overwhelmed by a line of questioning, that is perfectly okay. Instead of shutting things down with "whatever," simply express what is going on. "I'm a little overwhelmed with this conversation; can we come back to it later tonight after I've given it some thought" is a great example of showing your partner respect while also taking the time needed to process the situation.

FORGETTING IMPORTANT DETAILS OF CONVERSATIONS

If you aren't listening, then it is hard to remember all the important details of the conversation. When other people talk to you, whether it is your partner or someone else, they usually want to share information with you. Sure, some conversations are about having fun and talking, but often important information is shared during a conversation. When you ignore those details and forget about the important parts of the conversation, it appears to the other person like you don't care about what they have to say.

There will be times when you are worn out and tired, making the act of listening especially hard because all you want to do is take a nap. But if you want to keep important people in your life, then you need to pay attention to the details. Men, step up and practice some of your active listening skills to make this easier. If you struggle with attention and memory, try writing down notable bits of information, using the voice memo feature on your phone, or setting calendar reminders when key dates are mentioned.

IGNORING TEXTS
UNTIL IT'S TOO LATE

Texting is one of the biggest forms of communication used in our modern world. This allows us to get information back and forth to one another, without having to worry about whether the other person is available to pick up a phone. For many people, the ability to text can allow them to say things that they may not say otherwise or that they may worry about someone else overhearing.

When you are in a relationship, you will probably utilize text quite a bit. This is a simple form of communication to share information, such as reminding your partner to pick up some milk on their way home or asking how their day has gone. While someone may not be able to answer the text right at that moment, they can look when it is most convenient for them and answer in their own time.

Even if you don't expect your partner to respond back to the text right at that moment, if they choose s to ignore your text until it's too late for the response to matter, it can be annoying at best and harmful at worst. For example, maybe you wanted to invite them out for the night, but they chose to wait until the night was almost over before responding. While this could be a frustrating instance, not answering your text about getting locked out of the house can be more serious.

While bad texters have a million excuses for their unresponsiveness (they didn't see it or notice it), when you text them to pick up milk at 9 in the morning and they aren't home until 6 that night, you know that they chose to ignore it.

If there are certain times of day where you can't look at your phone at all, simply lay this boundary out with the women in your life. There doesn't need to be a difficult or rude conversation about it. Just simply express what times you can look at your phone and make sure to follow through with the set times.

CHAPTER FOUR:
KITCHEN CHRONICLES

Now, it's time for us to move into the kitchen. This is a magical place where yummy food is made, and memories can be shared with everyone in the family. However, it's common for the women of the home to feel like they spend an inordinate amount of time in this room just trying to keep it clean. They know that they clean up after they are done making a meal, but the second they let the man of the house in that room, all chaos breaks loose.

Men, it is time to step up in the kitchen. Not only should you be the one sharing in the duties of making the meals, but you should not leave a mess behind for someone else to clean up. The kitchen gets messy enough; try to work to keep it a little cleaner and looking nicer. Here are just a few things that men tend to do in the kitchen that can drive women crazy:

THE MAGICAL DISHWASHER THAT DOES NOT UNLOAD ITSELF

The dishwasher is one of the most amazing machines to come into the kitchen. No longer do people need to stand in the kitchen, fighting about who will need to clean all the dirty dishes. Instead, you can work together and fill up the dishwasher in a matter of minutes, and then walk away and relax while the machine does all the work.

When the dishwasher is done, you may be amazed at how sparkly and wonderful the dishes look. However, one thing the dishwasher is not able to do is put the dishes away for you.

You eat off the plates and dirty up the silverware, so take some responsibility and help empty the dishwasher. If the other person in the home already did the work of making supper, cleaning up, and putting all the dishes into the machine, then it is time for you to step up and do some of the work as well.

Nothing is more frustrating than trying to fill up the machine again and finding all the clean dishes in there. This means that the person trying to use the dishwasher will have to put them all away before they can finish the chore. If they reach into the machine to grab one dish because all of them were left there, it is likely they will just finish the chore that wasn't their responsibility in the first place.

Share in some of the burden. If you open the dishwasher to grab something out to use it, take the time to unload the rest of the dishes too. It only takes you a few minutes and shows that you are ready to be a partner and can take on some of the chores yourself.

THE ART OF
"I'LL DO IT LATER"

You may have the best intentions when you promise to do something later, but we all know how quickly those good intentions can falter. Maybe you are tired, or the kids want your attention. Maybe you just assume you will actually have more motivation and energy to clean up the mess in the kitchen later.

The problem is, later never seems to come. You forget about it or just decide to not bother with the mess at all. This may be great for you, since now you don't need to step up and do the work at all. But it is not great for the person who runs across the mess later and must deal with it all on their own.

Nothing is worse than walking into a kitchen the morning after the man of the house cooked a meal only to find the mess from last night never got taken care of. Cleaning up a whole kitchen mess in the morning, when everything has had a chance to sit on the plates and get stuck, can be a horrible way to wake up in the morning. It takes twice as long to clean up and will lead to a very angry cohabitant. If the woman of the house is a stay-at-home-mom or working from home while her partner goes to the office, this burden can feel even more unfair because she has to suffer from someone else's mess.

You will not magically find the motivation to clean up the mess later. Instead of hoping for that magic pill that gets you up and moving, choose to just get the work done now. It likely won't take you longer than ten minutes, and you can save a lot of headaches down the line. In general, practicing cleaning as you cook is the best way to keep anyone from feeling taken for granted later.

REFRIGERATOR TETRIS

Although completing stacking puzzles is a great skill to have for some things, it is not so great when the habit makes it impossible to find anything in the fridge. Men seem to find it funny to store things every which way in the fridge and hope for the best later.

The irony is, men are usually the ones struggling to find common items such as the ketchup, never mind the leftovers from three weeks ago stashed in the back.

It is nice that guys seem to want to help and lend some support, but when the fridge is a mess, there are a few problems. First, you need to worry about everything falling when you open the door. Sure, it's nice that supper was put away, but if it falls on the ground when the kids open the door, that leads to a huge mess that now needs to be cleaned up.

The second problem is that less will fit in the fridge if someone just chooses to throw things in without a care in the world. It may seem quicker to you, but when you cram 30 things into a fridge that only fits 20, there's a problem. This mess makes it hard to find just about anything, causing the woman of the home to just give up and reorganize everything herself.

In addition to the frustrations, a disorganized fridge increases food waste. Instead of being able to clearly see what needs to be eaten, items can easily be forgotten in the mess. In addition to this, you or your partner might buy double of an item you already have.

When you do add something to the fridge, take the time to store it properly. Stacking things nicely on top of one another and making sure that everything is upright and easy to see can make a difference in what the fridge can hold and how neat it looks.

LEAVING CRUMBS EVERYWHERE

Crumbs are small but add up quick. Sure, some foods can be a bit messy and tend to leave more behind than the rest, but does it need to always look like someone purposefully left a trail behind them? Nothing ruins a clean kitchen faster than a crumbly mess spread out over its surfaces.

Crumbs can be annoying. They are hard to get off the counter, usually requiring the use of a broom and dustpan or a wet cloth. Unless there is a proud two-year-old around who is learning how to do things for themselves, there's really no reason the house should be covered in crumbs.

To start, take the time to limit crumbs as much as possible while you're eating. Lay down a paper towel, a plate, or something else that will help to gather the crumbs and keep your counters as clean as possible. This makes it easier for you to clean up and limits the chance that you will leave a mess behind for someone else to take care of.

If you do happen to leave a few crumbs from your kitchen fun, then clean them up. A quick brush of the crumbs into your hands and then over to the trash only takes a few minutes, but it will save you and the woman of the house trouble later.

NOT WIPING
UP SPILLS

Spills are a part of life; they happen and are not usually a big deal. The trouble starts when someone fails to take the time to clean up after their spill. This simple spill, which only takes a few seconds to get off the floor or counter, now becomes a big mess that someone else must deal with.

If the liquid is freshly spilled, then there is the potential that someone will slip on it and fall. This may result in someone getting hurt. If the liquid has had time to dry, it may be sticky, which can make it hard to get off the counter or floor. This is especially common for refrigerator spills, which can mold, contaminate food, or harden if left unattended.

Unless you are two years old, you really shouldn't be leaving the mess until later. You are not a child, so take the time to clean it all up. There are likely some paper towels, napkins, or dish clothes close by in the kitchen. Grab one and clean up the mess before you turn around and go on with the rest of your day.

OVERFILLING THE
TRASH BIN

The dreaded trash can. It's full of all the trash from the day and it is there to make it easier to take it out. Of course, it can be a mess, and no one really enjoys the chore of taking out the trash. However, getting this done can keep the home fresh and clean. While you don't need to take it out every hour, you also need to use caution about letting it get too full on you.

Letting the trash get too full may not seem like a big deal, but when this happens, it is usually the woman of the home that ends up taking the trash bag out in the end. A heavy trash bag is never a good thing for the following reasons:

- The bag will become too heavy to be lifted out.
- The bag will split open, and its disgusting contents will go everywhere.
- Bad smells will build up and start to spread through the kitchen.
- You're more likely to have leaks or spills.

You can imagine just how happy your partner will be when this happens, all because you were too lazy to take out the trash.

While you can't be a mind reader, and you may not know when the trash is getting full, you can take some proactive steps to check on it. For example, the trash can is usually fullest at the end of the day, when everyone is done eating, and the area has been cleaned up. Look at the bag, and if it looks relatively full at the time, then take it on outside and replace it with a new one!

THE EVER-GROWING
PILE OF DISHES

After a long day of work, one of the last things that you want to think about is that growing pile of dishes in the sink. Maybe there are some breakfast and lunch dishes already in there. Add in the supper dishes, and the sink is starting to look full.

Do not leave that growing pile of dishes for someone else to deal with each day. If the dishes have been there since breakfast, or even from the day before, then they need to get cleaned.

If possible, offer to do the dishes when you start to see the pile growing. This will get you a ton of appreciation and can help keep the dishes manageable. It's the least you can do given all the other work that your partner puts in during the year to make life nice for you. If the pile of dishes is tall and you are worried about getting it all done on your own, consider whether you can work together. Just make sure you do the dirty part and let her worry about the drying and putting away!

COOKING WITH
EVERY POT AND PAN

You finally give in and promise to make that meal your partner will love. Whether it is a romantic gesture, or because your partner has finally lost it and refused to make the meal that night, it doesn't matter. Your lady is ready to sit back and enjoy whatever it is you decided to create in the kitchen.

After the meal is done, she walks into the kitchen and stares in amazement. Not at the culinary masterpiece that is in front of you, but at the sheer number of plates, bowls, pots and pans, and everything else that is scattered all around the kitchen. The dishes for this simple meal, which only needed one pan at most, will take hours to complete.

They are now shooting daggers at you, and you can't figure out why they aren't proud of you for making the meal. Instead of gratitude, your met with quiet resentment (at best). Whereas you saved them an hour of cooking, you've created three to four hours of work for them.

Men, while it is appreciated that you took the time to make a meal, you did not need to make such a mess. There isn't a single dish in the world that requires the use of everything in the kitchen, and most of them can be done with just one or two.

Before you jump in and start to make that next meal, consider how much cleaning up you would like to do afterwards. Do you really want to clean ten pots, twenty pans, and fifty plates after cooking a meal? Neither does your partner. Find a more efficient way to cook and save the mess and hassle. As mentioned before, emptying the dishwasher before you start and cleaning as you go is the easiest way to ensure a culinary success with an easy clean up after.

CHAPTER FIVE:
ENTERTAINMENT
ETIQUETTE

The question of who's in control of home entertainment can be an important part of any relationship. Whether you are choosing a movie to enjoy together or need to find a show out of the countless options, there are plenty of chances for the two of you to get into an argument about what to watch. Let's take a closer look at some of the entertainment etiquette mistakes men tend to make that will drive their partners crazy.

THE REMOTE-CONTROL MONOPOLY

Hoarding the remote control can be annoying and forces the other person to be a victim of whatever type of show the other person chooses to watch.

Remote control monopoly happens when one person in the relationship takes the remote and doesn't give it up. They will choose the show or movie to watch, how loud the volume is, and when it is time to change the program. If you are the person without the remote, it can be frustrating to get stuck with someone else having all the control.

Maybe the day will come when your partner doesn't feel like choosing the entertainment. They are tired and don't want to think about what to watch or how to control things. On those evenings, you can be the king of the castle and choose what you would like. However, you can score some extra points by taking the time to pick something your partner would like or something you can both watch together.

On most evenings though, you need to share the remote. The two of you live in the same place, or are at least spending the time together, so both should be able to enjoy what is on the TV. If you take control too often, it can cause anger and resentment. Offer the remote to your partner and let them pick the show on occasion.

MULTI-TASKING: MOBILE, TABLET, AND IGNORING THE WIFE

When you get to the end of the night, you want to spend some time with the one you love. You have both had busy days full of action, and now it is time to sit down, talk, and spend time with one another, hopefully without the kids bouncing all around. It is likely that your partner would love a chance to tell you something about their day or just have you listen to them. But if your nose is in those devices, then they will feel like you are ignoring them.

Many men fall into the habit of sitting down at night and then multi-tasking. We're not talking about the good kind of multi-tasking that allows for increased productivity and helpfulness. We're talking about the multi-tasking that takes over all the electronic devices in the home and blocks out the rest of the family completely.

Many men state that they aren't good at doing more than one thing at a time. But the fact that they have a show playing on the TV, they're engrossed in their social media feed, and are having a full conversation with several of their friends over text tends to undermine this claim. The only thing men seem incapable of doing at this point is paying attention to their wives.

With all these devices vying for attention at once, the wife may try to start the communication. It may not be critical, important information at that moment (though of course, how would you know if you are not paying attention?), but this doesn't mean that she isn't looking for some validation or a better response than a few grunts. She knows when she is being ignored and it is not a good feeling at all.

Put down the devices and spend some time listening to your wife. Yes, you may be tired and need to unwind, but choosing to have a million screens in front of your face is not helping you relax in the first place. In fact, it is setting you up for a big fight later on that will definitely make it hard for the two of you to get any sleep. Even if it is just five to ten minutes before you put on a show, take the time to give your wife some attention and hear more about her day.

ENDLESS CHANNEL SURFING

Pick a program already! Yes, there are often a lot of choices, but watching the TV switch from one show to the next can be annoying and enough to give anyone a headache if they are not careful.

Channel surfing should not become an extreme sport when you sit down with your partner to watch something. You should have a good idea of what you would like to watch with them before you even sit down. You likely have a list of favorite shows. Even on a streaming service, you can take a few minutes and type in a genre to narrow down some of the choices.

ADJUSTING VOLUMES TO THEATER LEVELS

There is something magical about the theater. The tasty popcorn, the excitement about seeing a movie you have been waiting to see a long time, and the darkness in the room. One thing that stands out about the theater experience as well is the booming volume that gives you a chance to feel like you are in the middle of all the action.

However, your home is not a movie theater, and you should not try to raise the volume to theater levels. Whether you live in an apartment or a house, be mindful of the amount of noise that you make when you turn on any station.

Hopefully, you aren't hard of hearing. While the loud noise can help make sure that you never miss a thing, it can also be tough on the ears. Protect your hearing and keep the volume down. Protect your sanity and don't wake up the kids with the loud noise in the middle of the night. Find a lower volume that is comfortable for everyone and use that as your basis to have an enjoyable experience. If you do struggle with your hearing, instead of cranking the sound up to accommodate hearing loss, try using subtitles as an aid instead.

HOGGING THE GAME CONSOLE

Gaming can be a fun pastime, a way to unwind at the end of the day and engage in play. But when you hog the gaming console the whole time, it can lead to disaster. You are not a five-year-old with a toy who doesn't want to share. Keep in mind that there are others around who might like to play.

Maybe your partner is into gaming and would like a chance to play with you (or on her own). Share the gaming experience and make it a time to spend with one another. If you have kids, maybe they want a chance to play some of the games as well. Even if no one else is interested in playing a game, when you hog the gaming console, you aren't sharing your attention with anyone else in the home.

This doesn't mean you need to give up your gaming fun all the time. But it does require you to become more in tune with what others need and to remember you are not the only person in the home. If you do decide to game, set a timer to limit yourself. When that timer goes off, it is time to check in with your loved ones and see if they want a turn or some attention.

GIVE AWAY
SPOILERS

No matter how much you may try, when you hear about a new spoiler, you want to share it with someone else. If this happens just a few minutes before the other person finds out, then it likely will not be as big of a deal because you can hold it in. But if you learn about spoilers well before your partner, you might let something slip and ruin your partner's viewing experience.

When it comes to watching a special event or looking up spoilers, you and your partner should be able to share the experience together. If they asked you to wait and watch a show with them, then be respectful enough to do this. They are looking forward to spending some extra time with you, and if you skip ahead and leave your partner behind, you will miss out on all the wonder that comes with watching together. It may be hard to wait all day, but you will make your partner happy and can create a great experience for the two of you to enjoy together.

OVER-INVITING
BUDDIES FOR GAMES

The big game is about to come on, and you are excited to have your buddies over to enjoy it. You have planned a great barbecue, you have all the drinks, and Steve is going to make his famous dip that everyone talked about from last time. It will be perfect—this is how great memories are made.

Your partner seemed to enjoy the last party and gets along well with your buddies, so why not invite them over for the next game, and then the next. Why not invite them over for every game for the rest of the season? A big party every week sounds just like what your social life needs right now.

But after you do this a few times, you notice that your partner is a little upset. What could have gone wrong?

While there is nothing wrong with having your buddies over on occasion to watch important games, no one wants to have a big crowd over at their home once or twice a week. It takes a lot of work to prepare for a party. Your partner likely cleans the home (both before and after your friends are there), gets the food, and plays hostess the whole time. This is a lot of work, and it can get exhausting.

There may be some weeks that your partner just wants to sit back and relax with you. There is something fun about just sitting around with your family in your sweatpants while you watch the game, rather than having to get everything cleaned up and ready to go. On the other hand, maybe she doesn't want to watch the game, and instead, just wants to relax for one night. If you're inviting all your buddies over every night, it is going to result in some problems.

Consider whether your partner is up for some of the extra work and don't let the buddies come over every night. Even better, any time you're planning a big event with *your* friends, take responsibility for the cleaning, cooking, hosting, and entertainment yourself! Let the lady in your life treat herself or spend time with her friends, while you handle your party on your own.

CHAPTER SIX:
AUTOMOTIVE ANTICS

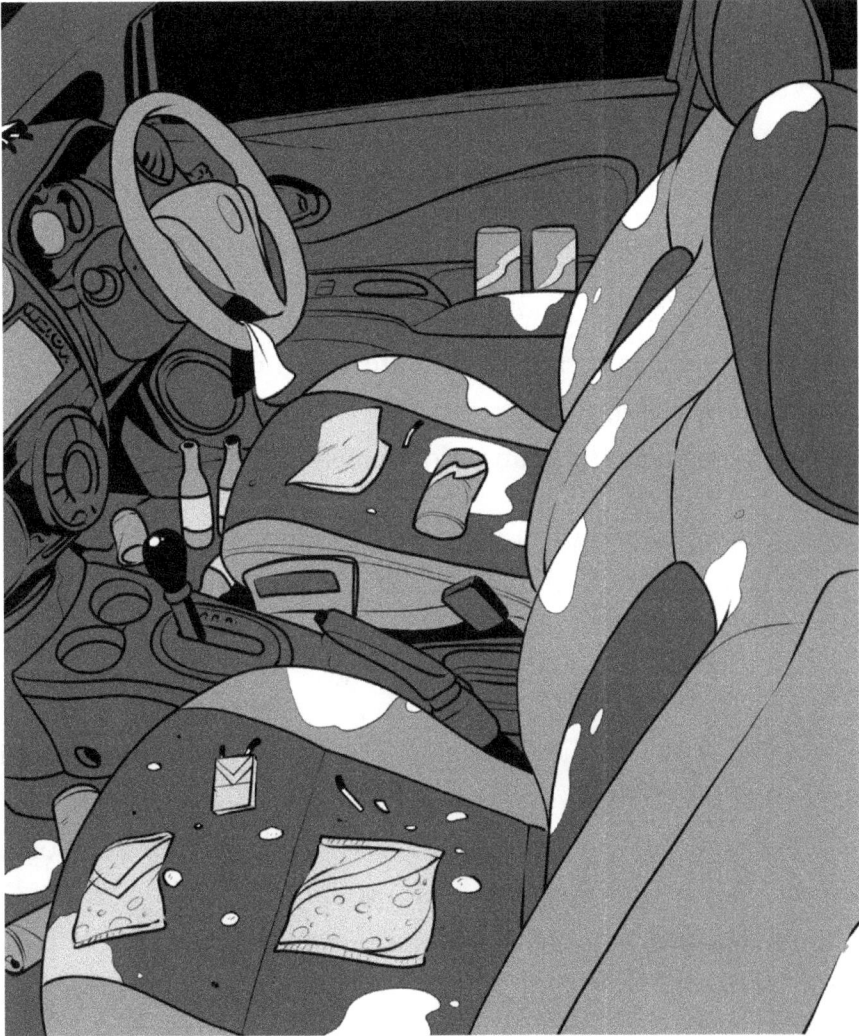

Now it's time to move on to some of the shenanigans that tend to happen in the car. Depending on how you drive, your lady will encounter a variety of different issues when it comes to vehicles. Whether you refuse to get directions on the next road trip, or they find that you have a whole wardrobe in the back of the vehicle, here are some of the top issues that your partner may deal with when it comes to a man's car.

THE "DECORATIVE" FUEL GAUGE

The fuel gauge is not supposed to be decorative. It is a tool in the car that is meant to be useful for telling you when it is time to fill up the tank again. But when the man of the relationship does not take care of it, the gauge can become obsolete.

There should not be a ton of lights on the dashboard. These are signs that something is going wrong with the vehicle and that you need to get it fixed. Ignoring these can be a bad idea, and you may end up stranded on the side of the road.

At best, the lights on the fuel gauge show you that it is time to fill up the gas tank before you go much further. When the light comes on, it's a sign that you need to get to a gas station as soon as possible. While you won't end up on the side of the road in the next few minutes, waiting until the gas light comes on to fill up the tank is risky and inefficient.

At worst, these "decorations" and lights are going to be signs that something serious is about to happen with the vehicle. Men, when you see these lights on the dash, it means it is time to get the issue fixed rather than ignoring it.

Even better, make a habit of topping off the fuel tank before your partner gets into the car. She might not anticipate a stop off for gas on her way to work. Leaving it up to her can make her late and add unnecessary stress to her day.

"I DON'T NEED DIRECTIONS"

We've all gotten lost on a long road trip. Even with good directions from a friend or the help of a map, we somehow get off the right path and are not able to get back on it. This is less likely to happen thanks to GPS and our smartphones, but if the directions are confusing or your phone is low on battery, you can still get lost.

Many men have too much pride to stop at a gas station or somewhere else to ask for directions. They assume that if they just keep following the same directions or going down the same path a little bit longer, then they will be able to get there and won't need to rely on someone else for help at all.

However, the reality of the situation never goes as planned. No matter how good of a navigator the man may think he is, once he is lost, he can waste precious time wandering around. Often this leads to a fight as the wife will try to convince her husband to stop for some help, which often causes the husband to double down on his pride and stubbornness. This can lead to an argument that ruins the whole road trip for everyone.

The best way to solve this problem is to ask for directions at the first sign of confusion. Maybe you get lucky, and your GPS and phone get you to the right location without a lot of problems. But if you feel like you are going around in circles and not getting to your destination, then it is time to swallow some of that pride and ask someone for help.

USING THE CAR
AS A SECOND CLOSET

While men may find it more convenient to just throw an old shirt in the back of the car or change in the garage instead of bringing everything inside, this is a bad idea. First, this leaves your car full of old, smelly clothes that could have the car stinking for months to follow. No wonder your partner never wants to take your car to the restaurant or airport and keeps handing over air fresheners as a sign that you need to make some changes.

Your car is not a second closet, and leaving items in there is not a good idea. They will get wrinkly and old, making it hard for you to wear them again, even if you keep them there for a long time. All those clothes limit the amount of space in the car, making it hard if you need to pick up something for your partner or have someone ride in the back seat. If you stuff enough clothes in there, you will run out of things to wear inside the home.

Rather than changing in the garage or throwing items off and into the back of the car, bring them all in. Better yet, change in the home and then take the clothes right to the laundry room instead. This will keep your car clean, help you find some of the clothes you need, and even save your partner a trip picking the items up themselves.

REFUSING TO CLEAN OUT THE BACKSEAT

Even if you manage to keep the back seat free of clothes, it is possible that the car has a good deal of trash and other items lying around. The backseat of a vehicle is not meant to be a second trash can. Sure, you may have a long trip and end up leaving some things back there until you get home. However, you should not let the trash accumulate and build up over time; it can get disgusting, and no one likes to open their car door only for junk to fall out.

There is nothing less romantic than your partner having to wade through a sea of energy drink cans, coffee cups, and take out bags to ride in the passenger seat. Even worse is when there's not enough room for them to comfortably place their feet on the ground at all. Chances are, if your car is a mess, your partner will get frustrated enough to do something about it for you.

This may seem like a win. You don't have to do any of the work to clean up the vehicle, but it still gets cleaned out. Even if your partner says they don't mind, cleaning up after an adult gets old and leaves people feeling taken for granted. It's better to get in the habit of keeping a small bag for trash in the car and to stay on top of it. If you have kids, this is extra important as they'll come with their own messes and need a clean space to sit when riding with you.

OVERESTIMATING PARKING SKILLS

Every man likes to talk a big game about how they're the ultimate parking machine. There is no spot too small and no area too complicated that they are not able to fit into. They may have a small car that is easy to maneuver around or a big truck that takes a bit more skill. However, they always have the confidence that they can make it happen and get the closest parking spot possible each time they drive around.

The problems arise when they start to overestimate their parking skills. Sure, you may be pretty good at parking, but that doesn't mean you should pass up the ten great parking spots that are already available, only to get a few steps closer to the building. Everyone can handle a little bit of walking; if you keep messing around, those good parking spots will be gone, and you will be forced to park even further away.

Overestimating the amount of space available in a spot can cause some problems as well. Even if it is the best parking spot in the world, if it is meant for a compact car and you are driving a big truck, then you just won't fit. It isn't about your parking skills, it's about the size of the vehicle you are messing with. Trying to get that spot will anger the people in the car with you, everyone else trying to drive around you, and may even result in an accident.

Admit that you are not a "parking ninja" when the odds are stacked against you. Graciously offer to take one of the other spots that your partner has been pointing out for you, coming in as the good guy along the way. Then get out and enjoy your day.

PROCRASTINATING VEHICLE MAINTENANCE

We get this one a little bit. No one really wants to head to the mechanic shop and find out that they need to dump hundreds or thousands of dollars into their vehicle. But when your dashboard is lit up so much that it looks like a Christmas tree, the situation is starting to border on the ridiculous.

Your partner does not want to receive a call that you are on the side of the road because your car finally broke down when they told you to take it in six months ago. They also don't want to be with you when this happens and have to wait for a tow truck to come. Sure, the costs can be high, but this is why you take the time to budget and plan for it.

The cost of owning a car means that you need to be ready for some of the expenses that may come along the way. This includes regular maintenance. When you see some of those pretty lights start to show up, then get the car to your mechanic and see what is wrong. It will most likely cost you a lot less compared to waiting longer and making the situation worse.

There are also some vehicle maintenance actions that you can take along the way, before little issues turn into bigger problems. Changing the oil, rotating the tires, and having a tune-up on occasion will make a difference and can prolong the life of your car.

BLASTING THE AC OR HEAT WITHOUT ASKING

Before messing with the dials in the vehicle, check with your partner. It's a small gesture that can mean a lot. If they're cold, and you blast the AC, they might not say anything, but they'll feel it and remember why they don't like riding with you.

Likewise, if you are borrowing or sharing a vehicle, make sure to return the settings to where they were. The last thing anyone wants to experience is to get into a freezing or uncomfortably hot vehicle when they are not prepared for it, especially early in the morning.

Taking the time to consider your partner's needs is a habit that stacks up brownie points over time. Your partner might not notice the small gesture at first, but they'll certainly notice when they are uncomfortable.

CHAPTER SEVEN: SHOPPING SAGAS

When it is time to go shopping, it often seems like couples will get into some of the worst fights. One party or the other will want to spend more time shopping or will decide to make more purchases than the other, and often one of the partners doesn't want to be there in the first place. This can lead to several bad behaviors between the two of them that can turn what could be a fun experience into a bad one.

In this chapter, we are going to look at some of the things that men do during a shopping trip that can be enough to drive their partner up a wall.

SPEED-SHOPPING

It's almost as if the floor is lava and will burn you up in two seconds if you do not make it through the store quickly enough. Your partner isn't quite sure what they are in such a hurry about. Sure, they have no desire to spend all day at the store, but that doesn't mean this shopping trip needs to turn into a speed racing adventure either.

Speed shopping is something that should only happen when you have an actual emergency and need to grab a handful of things. However, for most shopping trips, rushing through things increases the stress on your partner. Slowing down can help make the experience smoother.

Nothing is worse than trying to get the items you need on your list and having someone beside you trying to make you hurry a little faster. Pressuring your partner to get out faster can increase brain fog, make decision making difficult, and generally make the chore that much more annoying. Sure, something like grocery shopping isn't all that exciting to start with. However, if you are out and about for fun or looking for gifts, then all the magic is gone when you are rushed.

Men, it is time to take a step back and learn to stop rushing your partner. If they want to take some extra time at the store, then let them. You can speed through things as much as you want on your own time. But when you agreed to go with your partner to the store, you agreed to go at their speed. If you find the way they shop is tedious, then offer to take over the task entirely instead.

THE "IT'S ON SALE" JUSTIFICATION

Many families are on a budget. With prices rising faster than anything, it is harder than ever to find all the items that you need and ensure they fit in your family's budget. While your wife may wish there was enough money to go out and enjoy a good shopping trip, they have held back and sacrificed to make sure that the important things in the budget are covered.

This is why it is always so frustrating when the husband comes to the store and adds in a bunch of things that were not on the list, saying that he needs to get them because "it's on sale." Yes, there may be a great deal on that item, but if it was not on the list and not in the budget, then the item is not something that should end up in the cart.

Before walking into the store, it is a good idea to have a list and a budget, and then stick to it. Stores are good at putting up sales and placing items so that they are enticing when you walk in the door. However, you are a grown-up and should know enough to avoid falling for these gimmicks. Learn how to stick to your budget, and if you expect your wife to say "no" to things, then you need to say "no" to them too.

FORGETTING THE PRIMARY ITEM

When you head to the store, there is often one main item that you really need to get. If you go for yourself, forgetting that item may not be a big deal. However, when you head to the store to pick up a few items for your wife or family, forgetting to pick up that certain something can cause an unpleasant surprise when you return empty-handed.

There is usually a good reason that your wife sent you to the store to grab a few items. It isn't just for your health and rarely is it to get you out of the house. It is often an item that they need right away, perhaps for the kids or to complete supper. Otherwise, they could wait and go get the item later when they have some more time.

Maybe you got to the store and got distracted. You decided to grab a few of your own items and promised to go back and get the item that your wife asked for before you leave the store. However, you get so distracted grabbing your stuff, talking to the sales associate, and perhaps running into an old friend, that you forget about the key purchase.

When you get back to the house, your wife realizes that you did not pick up the one or two items she had asked you to grab in the first place. Now dinner is delayed, or the kids don't have that important item they need to finish their school project. Your wife is mad and either sends you back to the store, trusting you will remember things this time, or she'll run to the store on her own. This slows things down, adds plenty of frustration, and puts you in the doghouse for the rest of the night.

If your wife or partner sends you to the store to grab something, then you need to make sure that you come up with that item. Even if you forget all the things that you needed to grab from the store, you better come home with the item your spouse needs. Write a list with the item, send yourself a message, or do something so that there is no chance you will forget next time.

AVOIDING THE "FEMININE PRODUCTS" AISLE

For some men, this is the scariest aisle in the whole world. It is worse than going to a scary movie or having to clean up around the house. While it is a perfectly natural process for women, these men are not going anywhere near it, no matter how much it could help their spouse or partner out.

The feminine products aisle is not a place to fear. Given how much your partner does for you, you can take a few minutes to do something helpful for her too. If she needs you to run in and grab some feminine products, then get in there and do it.

While it may feel a little awkward and uncomfortable at first, you will get used to it. We promise that no one is really paying that much attention to you anyway when you are in there. In addition, you can be the hero for your partner if you are able to get to the aisle and just pick out the right products, without them needing to even ask. Bonus points if you keep an emergency stash for her just in case she runs out when no one can get to the store or starts unexpectedly while out in public.

ADDING UNNECESSARY GADGETS TO THE CART

There are so many random things that you can find in a store, and it seems that many husbands are just like kids; they gravitate to the stuff that is useless. No wife wants to feel like the mother when they enter the store, but when they start to see all the unnecessary gadgets that find their way into the cart, it's no wonder that they start to get frazzled.

Unless there is a specific use for an item, it does not need to find its way into the cart. This is where that list can be useful before you get into the store. The two of you can sit down and write out a list of what you need and then no one is allowed to depart from it, no matter how enticing all the other items are in the store. This can keep you on budget and prevent an argument in the store.

LOSING PATIENCE IN CHECKOUT LINES

For most stores, the checkout lines are quick. Stores are getting better at having enough employees present to handle some of the customers that come in, and with the self-checkout in some stores, the process can go even faster.

However, there are those days of the year when shopping can take longer than usual. Saturdays are notoriously bad when you need to hit one of the stores to pick up something, especially when you need to get a full load of groceries. It will seem like everyone else in the town is out with the same idea as you.

Other times, the cashier in the line you choose can be one of the slowest workers around. You may have gotten into the short line with only a few people and not that many items, but you are still standing in the same place twenty minutes later.

Sure, this is frustrating. But it's not like your wife doesn't realize this as well. She is likely frustrated with the situation too. The difference is that she knows how to act in public and won't try to make a scene because of the amount of time that is slipping by. She understands that things take time, and eventually, you will get out of the store.

On the other hand, many men can't seem to hold onto their patience long enough to make it through this. They may start out with a few snide comments about how long it is taking and how they have better things to do. But if the line takes too long, then they can start to get more aggressive and angrier, causing a scene that is worse than a child's tantrum.

While it's fine to be frustrated about the checkout line, you are an adult and should know that waiting is part of life. Understanding that things take time and keeping your temper in check can make a difference. Find some way to entertain yourself and help during this time. If you really can't handle staying in the line any longer, offer to go and grab the car to make the journey easier for your wife when she is done and needs to load things up.

MISPLACING THE SHOPPING LIST

Your shopping list is one of the most important things that you will take to the store with you. Whether it was written down in just a few minutes before you were sent off to the store, or whether your wife took a few days to write it out, this list is an important tool for staying organized.

Many times, when you need to grab more than one thing at the store, having a list will make it easier to remember. Let's face it, if you are going to forget something at the store, it is often the one item that is the most important. A shopping list will make a difference in how smoothly shopping can go.

However, this won't work if you forget the list entirely. Now, you have to try and remember what is needed from memory, which is one of the worst things to happen when you are already panicking because you lost the list. Of course, you will forget half of it and have to head back to the store again.

There are ways to avoid this problem. Double check before you leave the house that you have the list in your hand. If you are worried you will forget the piece of paper or lose it in the car, take a picture of it on your phone. How often are you without that device? Then you can just pull up the picture and make sure you walk out of the store with everything you need.

COMPLAINING ABOUT MALL TIME

Whether you are going to the mall to get all that back-to-school shopping done, or you want to get a head start on some of your Christmas shopping, there are a million reasons to head to the mall. The man agreed to come along for the ride, but now that you both are there, all he wants to do is complain about how long it is taking.

Malls are big places. If you are just wandering around and spending some time together, there shouldn't be a rush to get it all done. Men, pushing the woman in your life along and complaining when she wants to go into a few stores can make things turn sour quickly. This might be her one time to get out of the house and away from the kids, or maybe she was excited to spend time with you. No matter the cause, your whining is not winning you any favors and may make things miserable the next time you want to have her come along to do something.

If you are there to get some back-to-school shopping or holiday shopping done, then the complaining can be even worse. Everyone is already stressed out enough, trying to beat the other shoppers and find everything on a time limit. Not only is your whining annoying, but it's going to make the situation worse, and she is going to snap at you pretty soon.

Rather than being a pain about the mall, see if there are some ways you can help. When the whole family is along, help look for some of the items or offer to go to one or two of the stores while your partner is busy in another one. This can take some of the pressure off her and speed up the process. If you are there just to spend some time with one another, turn off your phone and ignore the time because your attention should just be on your partner and the time you are spending together now.

CHAPTER EIGHT: TECHNOLOGICAL TANGLES

Technology is amazing, enabling us to do things that we never thought possible before. However, there are also components of this technology that can slow us down and make it difficult for two partners in a relationship to get along and do well together. In particular, there are a few ways that men can act around technology that will drive their partners crazy. Let's dive into some of these and see what we can learn!

OVERDOING THE "TURN IT OFF AND ON AGAIN" METHOD

One of the best things that you can try when a device is no longer working is to turn it off and back on. This is a simple method that essentially restarts the device and may even bring in prompt some updates. However, if you have done this method once, there isn't much of a need to do it again and again.

It can get annoying when the man of the house tries to turn the device on and off, hoping for a different result than what they were able to get before. If it didn't work the first time, then it is unlikely that this method is going to work a few minutes later, no matter how many times you give it a try.

Technology can be complicated, and sometimes it takes a few different methods to get the right results. Men, if all else fails, give tech support a call (this may require you to swallow your pride a little bit), and see how they can help you with your device.

TECH
HOARDING

Tech hoarding could be taking over your life. If you have someone in the home who likes to go through a lot of devices, but never seems to throw them out, then tech hoarding can be a problem.

You do not need to leave 20 phones in the junk drawers, taking up space and leaving clutter. In one study done in 2021, it was estimated that only 19% of people admitted to recycling some of the electronics they no longer used. This means that there is technology piling up in their homes.

Your partner does not want to open the junk drawer and find a mess of other electronics in there. You need to take the time to get the important pictures and data off (which is much easier now that a lot of them have moved to the cloud storage, so your pictures follow you from one device to another), and then recycle the phone. This clears up room in your home and saves some fights.

SELECTIVE
NOTIFICATION
HEARING

Men seem to answer every notification that pops up on their screen. Their women can hear their phone beeping all the time and see they can't wait to start texting back, checking their social media account, or doing something else on their phones. Then when they send you a text or try to give you a call, you do not respond at all.

This is called "selective notification hearing." Whether you have seen that their message came through or not, it can be rude. You have time to look at the videos your friends send over, but you do not have the time to answer a quick text that they have sent to you. This is a quick way to show someone in your life where they rank on your scale of importance.

Men, if this is something that you do, then it is time to stop. Either turn off all the notifications and pay attention to what is going on around you or pay attention to all notifications equally. Whether it is an important message they need you to respond to immediately or they are just checking in, you can really show your spouse that you care by responding to them and not making them wait all the time.

INCESSANT GADGET UPGRADES

You do not need to upgrade your gadgets all the time. When you purchase one, the idea is generally to keep it for a couple of years. This is why many devices offer warranties to help you keep them in good shape for a few years. But when you think you need to get an upgrade all the time, it can get annoying.

The first issue is that this is a bit of a show-off move. It looks like you are just trying to show to others that you have the resources and status to constantly buy the latest upgrade. While a new device on occasion is not a big deal, if you are upgrading every few months, it will start to grate on others' nerves a little bit.

Another issue is the expense. Your spouse is not going to be happy if you keep telling her to watch the grocery bill or not spend extra on clothes, but then you turn around and spend as much as you want on new gadgets. Most of these cost a lot of money, even if you can get them for a good discount, so do not purchase them as often if you want to stick with a budget.

You do not need every upgrade that comes out. Sure, there may be a few little features that are different, but it often does not justify the cost. These upgrades are meant to entice customers who have not upgraded in a long time, not someone who just upgraded last month (though the tech companies aren't going to turn away your business if you are willing to pay). Make a commitment to not upgrade for at least two years and take good care of your current device. You will find that the lack of upgrading can save you money and you won't notice that your device is older when you let that go.

UNSOLICITED TECH-ADVICE

There are times when your partner will ask you to step in and provide them with some advice on their technical device. It could be that they need some advice on which new phone or tablet to get, or they need some troubleshooting help to handle some technical issues that come up. When these situations arise and they actively ask you for help, it can be nice when you are able to help them.

However, no one likes to get all that unsolicited tech advice along the way. It can be tedious and overwhelming for your partner to hear long rants about why they need to upgrade their phone or a long to do list on how to make their technology run faster. If they are already frustrated, this unsolicited monologue can feel overbearing at best.

Men, you need to know when to offer advice and when to leave it alone. You may be surprised at how annoying your unsolicited advice can be to someone, especially if they have heard it multiple times. Before giving advice, see whether the other person wants some of this help or not.

ENDLESS APP NOTIFICATIONS

While you can have as many apps on your phone as you would like, the notifications can be annoying to those who are around you. The constant dinging or beeps or vibrations from your phone can put a damper on pretty much any mood and distract from other important activities.

Our brains are programmed to answer all those beeps and dings. The app may just be a reminder to check it for that day. But no matter what it is, we won't know until we click on it and take a closer look. This can take your attention away from the other person or the task you committed to, which is rude and inconsiderate. This is especially troublesome when you are in the middle of a conversation and your phone starts exploding with notifications.

Even if you think you have some willpower, the moment that you hear that beep or ding, your mind will start to wander away from the conversation and will not come back until you can check the notification. The other person will notice that you have lost some interest in the conversation, and this can hurt their feelings as well.

There are a few ways to deal with this. First, keep the sound off on your phone. You can set up the phone so that it will still ring when someone calls, but other notifications are muted. This means that you will not hear when a notification comes up and will have to actively look at your phone to see if you've been notified. There are even ways to set time limits, so your phone is set to silent notifications while you are at home with your partner and family.

You can also limit the notifications that come through on the phone. You don't need to know everything that every app is always doing. If you get too many notifications, you can turn off notifications completely. Decide whether some of the apps are ones that you even use and consider erasing some to help limit notifications. Choose which ones are the most important to you.

LOUD PHONE CONVERSATIONS

Unless you are deaf, you do not need to have the volume turned way up on your phone, and you do not need to scream into your own phone either. This is bad etiquette and will get really annoying in no time (this also goes for video calls and Zoom meetings).

No one around you, whether it is your spouse, your kids, or someone who just happens to be walking by, wants to hear your phone conversation. When you insist on screaming into the phone, or you have the sound way up so everyone else can hear the other person, then you are going to get some stares. This goes double for when you are in an indoor public space, such as a restaurant, coffee shop, library, or grocery store.

The first thing to remember is that you don't need to shout into the phone. The person on the other side is probably tired of hearing your outdoor voice and has the volume turned down as much as possible to offset some of the noise. Phones are not some new-fangled inventions you have never used before; you have probably used one for years now. Talk normally on it and it is likely the other person will hear you just fine.

Next, you need to consider how loudly the other person is coming in as well. It is unlikely you need the speaker phone on when you are in public. You can do this in a car if you don't want to hold the phone or at home while doing other tasks. But when you are out there in public, you should turn the speaker phone off and the volume down. Always remember that the conversation should just be between the two of you, not everyone else. If you go any louder than that, it can cause problems.

OVER-RELIANCE ON VOICE ASSISTANTS

Don't get us wrong, there are some wonderful things that you can do with voice assistants. If you are in the middle of a meal and want to turn on some music, you can use your Echo to get it done. Using voice assistance to send a text while driving or looking up directions hands-free can be a safety thing as well. We aren't saying that men need to get rid of all the voice assistants and never use them, but we are saying that there is a benefit to doing some things on your own.

Men, you do not need to use voice assistants for everything. You can get up and turn down the thermostat on your own. You can type something into the TV to find the show that you want, rather than trying to talk to the remote. You don't need to rely on your Siri or Dot or another device to help you write a grocery list.

It can get annoying hearing all the commands that you send over to your voice assistant, not to mention that it is a little bit lazy. Technology is a great and wonderful thing that can make us more efficient. But when you are home, it may be best to leave some of these to a minimum and focus on doing some of the tasks on your own.

CHAPTER NINE: HOBBY HABITS

There is nothing wrong with having some hobbies to enjoy, and you should fully expect that your husband or partner will have some of his own. These hobbies allow both of you time to recharge and are a great way to spend some time apart doing the things you love. However, there are some "hobbies" that men can take on that end up causing more stress and headache for the women of the home than anyone else. In fact, they seem to be more excuses to clutter the home and spend money or get out of other projects. Let's look at some of those hobby habits that tend to cause problems.

THE INFINITE DIY PROJECT

It's nice that you want to spend some time fixing up the house, while saving money by doing the work yourself. The problem is when that project seems to take forever.

You start by hitting the project with gusto, working hard to get it all done and make it look amazing. The first week or so, everything comes down and that little part of the home that is getting the DIY treatment starts to look like a war zone. It may even look like you are making some good progress and may get the work done this time.

But then life gets in the way, boredom strikes, or you realize you don't have the tools or know-how to finish the job. Then you go back to work, and you foolishly think you will get some more done the next weekend. But then you decide to go out and play golf with some friends, or you need to pick up some special supplies out of town (and of course those just sit around for a long time and take up space).

Before you know it, the project that should have been done in a few weeks has been sitting there for six months, taking up space and aggravating the woman of the home. Every time she suggests getting someone in there to finish it, you get offended. After a while, she gives up and calls in a contractor who gets the work done in a fraction of the time, but probably for more money than it would have cost to just have the professional do it in the first place.

Men, if you promise to do a DIY project around the home, then make sure that you stick with it and get it done. Sure, you have work and a life and may not be able to make the same progress as a professional, but this is not an excuse to make commitments you can't keep. Have a plan in place from the beginning, get all the supplies, and knock it out as soon as possible.

GOLF IS JUST A SHORT GAME

Every time you head out for a game of golf, you promise that this one will be a quick one. You may try to sneak out before your spouse needs to go to work or promise it will be quick and then you can take the kids. But anyone who has ever played a round of golf knows that the games can get long. It is only the men who come home to find their wives about to lose their minds after being left alone with the kids all day that seem surprised by this.

It may start out innocently enough, but if someone was relying on you to get back to help with stuff around the home or to give them a break from the kids, then this lingering is not a good thing. It is disrespectful, and many times it results in the women feeling undervalued and unappreciated. It has nothing to do with you getting a break or spending time with your friends, but it is more the fact that they never got this break while you were gone all day long.

The next time you want to go play golf, make sure to plan it ahead of time. Even better, plan for the kids to go to grandma's house for the day so that both you and your partner can have a day off and not feel drained by the end. It is best to not assume the game will be quick, because things always have a way of getting out of control and then you will end up with an angry spouse when you get back.

OVERFLOWING
TOOL KITS

It isn't that you have the tools and a toolbox. In fact, it comes in handy on occasion when there are a lot of projects to get done around the house. The problem lies more with the fact that those extra tools seem to not have a home and get all over the place, rather than just staying in the box.

If you do insist on having that tool kit, then you need to make sure that everything has a place. This will keep the whole area more organized, making it less likely that you will misplace something important or that your spouse will trip over something and get hurt. Nothing is worse than getting started on a project and not being able to find the tool you need. This may result in the project not getting done or spending extra money just to find that the tool was lost in the garage.

Take the time to sort through your toolbox right now and see what belongs and what may need to be replaced. You may find that there are a few different tools in there that are the same or can do the same purpose. Hang them up, put them away, and find a space for everything to make it easier to find what you need the next time you work on a project.

Unless you are a contractor, there really is no reason for you to have an overflowing toolkit in the first place. You likely only need a few essential tools that will get the project started and will handle a lot of the work you would like to do around the home. Then, if you need something more specialized, you can always borrow or even rent the item to get the project done. Only purchase the item if you plan (and can stick to your plan) to use it often or if the rental amount for it is way too high.

NEW HOBBIES EVERY MONTH

A hobby is something that you decide to consistently spend your time on. It can help you feel accomplished, allows you to reach a goal, and can be a good way to relax. While there is nothing wrong with trying out a few new hobbies, "hobby shopping" can get annoying.

This is something that kids do; they jump from one hobby to another and don't stick with one thing that long. This can get annoying as your spouse tries to get it all scheduled into the calendar with their own commitments. If you insist on having new equipment or supplies for each hobby, it can start to cut into the family budget more than you can imagine.

If you want to start a new hobby, slow down before you try to jump into it without thinking. Do some research and talk to others to see if this is really something that you can see yourself doing. When you still feel like trying it out, start with some of the basics of it, and then try it a few times. If it is something that you decide to stick with, then you can slowly grow your collection, but if you do not enjoy it, then you don't waste the time and money.

A hobby is something that you are supposed to try for a longer period in order to really enjoy it and use it as a type of stress relief. It isn't really a hobby if you decide to change it monthly, and most new hobbies require investing time and practice in order to grow into a meaningful pastime. Men, unless you want your spouse to start going on big shopping trips each month or starting her own expensive hobbies all the time, it may be a better idea to just take it easy and stick with one thing for a longer period.

OVERBUYING FOR EACH NEW INTEREST

It is normal to be a little bit excited about a new hobby. You want to give it a try and are ready to give it your all as soon as possible. One of the first things that many men will do when they decide to get started with a new hobby is run to the store and see how many items they can purchase.

Rather than getting some of the basics for the hobby and seeing whether they will enjoy it or not, they will jump right in and buy everything they need (plus all the cool extras) before they have spent much time with the hobby.

Whether you stick with that hobby or not, this can be a risky move. You may not be certain how long you will do the hobby or whether you will stick with it. In some cases, when you work on a hobby, you may find that some items are not as necessary as you thought in the beginning. You may even give up on the hobby after just a few weeks, and now you have all those items sitting around gathering up dust for an activity you did not spend that much time on.

While one hobby can take up a ton of space around your home, think about what happens when you do five of these hobbies, or even more. As time goes on, you have spent a ton of money on hobbies that you aren't even engaging with, and your home is becoming a big mess in the process.

A better idea is to just get the basics. Take your time exploring a hobby and seeing if it is something that you will enjoy. When you are certain that this fits with your interests and will be fun, you can then take some time to purchase the bare necessities to get the hobby started. If you find that you enjoy the hobby, you can choose to ask for some more hobby-related items as gifts or slowly buy some more. But at least then you know it is a hobby you enjoy, and you will pick out the right items to make it more enjoyable.

IGNORING SAFETY INSTRUCTIONS

Many of the hobbies that you want to participate in will have some safety instructions that go with them. Even if they don't, you may need to use some caution along the way to be safe, such as when you are trying to play a sport.

Many men do not like to read instructions and assume they can figure everything out all on their own. But when you ignore the safety instructions, you will make the whole task more dangerous and less fun. Your spouse does not want to take you to the emergency room and foot a big bill on top of the money that she spent on getting the hobby started.

Before you get started with any new hobby, read any instructions to set yourself up for a safe and effective activity. Some items will come with a quick sentence on the box to help you use the items safely, and others will have more of a manual that you need to read through. Take the time to look through all of the safety instructions to make sure you can enjoy your new hobby.

You would want your kids to investigate all of the safety instructions to make sure that they don't do anything the wrong way. So, why won't you take the time to do it too? It only takes a few minutes to read the safety instructions, and you can really make sure that you are learning the hobby in the right way as safely as possible.

CLUTTERING SPACES WITH HOBBY MATERIALS

Your home is not meant to be a storage facility. While it's okay to keep a few items around here and there, it's not okay to have the remnants of 20 different hobbies abandoned around the house.

The first step to consider is that you should only purchase the items that you need for a new hobby and choose your hobbies carefully. But if you already have all those items from the different hobbies inside your home, it may be time to say goodbye to them and try a garage sale to recoup some of the money.

If you do have a few hobbies, take the time to clear up some space for the new items you need. You don't need to take up half the house with all your hobby materials, or you will end up with a mess on your hands. Your spouse will also be unhappy that she had to crawl over everything to get to the space she needs for something important.

Similar to how you would not like your spouse making a mess with their items, they don't want you to do the same. Think about the items you will need for that hobby and where you will put them ahead of time. If you don't have the room necessary for the new hobby, then it may be a good idea to either get rid of some of the old items you have from past hobbies or consider whether this is a hobby you want to start.

CHAPTER TEN:
FASHION FIASCOS

Some of the fashion choices that the men make can be questionable at best. Many will just focus on a pair of jeans and a few trusted shirts, or they may rely on their work dress code to help them know what is appropriate to wear. But for some men, the second they are allowed to choose some of their own clothing and outfits, it seems like they revert to childhood and have no idea what looks good on them. Let's take a closer look at some of the fashion fiascos that many men will cause when they try to dress themselves.

MISMATCHED SOCKS

When you purchase the socks at the store, they come in a pair. These two socks are meant to be friends, buddies, pals, and you are supposed to wear them together. Sometimes, you will get them all in white, so they are easy to match and won't take as long in the laundry as before. But other socks are designed to be colorful and go together, so it is important to match them.

Unless it is mismatched sock day at work, you need to take the time to match up your socks before you put them on. This does not mean you rely on your spouse to do the matching for you. Socks are easy to tell apart, and it won't take a lot for you to figure out whether the two socks in your hands go together or not.

Rather than just throwing on any two random socks and calling it a day (which looks bad and is thoroughly noticeable), take the time to sort through your socks and see which ones are meant to be worn together. You may have to search through the dryer a bit to help you find the right socks, but it does wonders for helping bring the outfit together.

OLD COLLEGE SWEATSHIRT LOYALTY

There is nothing wrong with being a fan of where you went to school. Your partner may even steal your sweater a few times to wear on their own and enjoy as well. But there comes a time when the sweater is all worn out and no longer looks very good. When that happens, it is time to throw the sweater out or find a creative way to preserve the memory.

Having a college sweater for a few years after you are done with school can be fun. Colleges make some nice sweaters that are great for curling up with when the weather turns cold, and you are worried about staying warm. But if it has been 20+ years since you went to college, that sweater is going to start looking ratty and you should not leave the house with it on any longer.

Once you can no longer recognize the emblem that is on the sweater, it is time to get rid of it. If you are really a fan of the school and still participate in the alumni network, then maybe consider purchasing a new one to keep the tradition going. But once it becomes an embarrassment to go out in public with that sweater, then it is time to give it a break.

Similar to all the clothes on this list, you will need to know when it is time to get rid of them and move on to something new. It may be hard to give up that sweater you have loved the last 20 years. However, we promise that the college store still has plenty for you to choose from. Go on a little shopping trip and purchase something nice for you and your spouse to help support your team!

HOLDING ONTO OLD JEANS

Nothing is better than finding that perfect pair of jeans. They are comfortable to wear, and you never want to take them off. They look amazing on you and ensure that you look your very best, no matter the occasion that you need to head out to for the day. You never want to let them go.

But like any pair of clothing, there will come a time when the jeans wear out and it's not a good idea to continue holding onto them longer than you should. At some point, there are too many holes in the jeans, too much of the fabric has worn out, and it is not a good idea to keep wearing them.

You can usually tell when this starts to happen. One little hole turns into a big one, and you discover a new rip or tear each time that you put them on. It may not seem like a big deal, but if you start to notice that your partner is cringing each time they see you wearing those particular pair of jeans, then it may be time to consider retiring them.

Depending on how often you wear the jeans, you may be able to extend their lifespan and keep them for many years. But if you wear them to work or keep them around for all those big events, then they will wear out faster. It's important to know when the jeans are worn out and need a break.

It is easy enough to get to the store and get a new pair of jeans. You don't have to stick with one pair; you can find a good pair of jeans for an affordable price. You just need to get off the couch and make that happen. Stop wearing those old jeans that no longer hold their shape or have holes and move on to something that is much better and makes you look nice.

INSISTING HATS HIDE BAD HAIR DAYS

The hat is an amazing invention. It can complement your outfit, protect you from the sun, and even hide a bad hair day.

Everyone has hidden difficult hair under a hat on occasion, but this is not an excuse to do this all the time. When you try to go through each day without taking care of your hair and assume that a hat will solve all the problems, you are going to run into some troubles.

Everyone can tell when you do this all the time, and the hat can often make the issue much worse than before. Take care of your appearance and make sure that you can wear something that looks nice. A hat can be a good way to hide a bad hair day when you have no time and no other choice, but it should not become your fallback option when you want to be lazy.

REPEATED FOOTWEAR

Finding a good pair of shoes can feel like heaven. They not only feel comfortable and can get you through work, school, and all your other obligations for the day, but they look amazing on you as well. If you have already taken the time to break them in, why would you want to go through all the effort again to find a new pair?

However, at some point, those beloved shoes are going to get worn out. You don't have to get rid of them right away, but when they are barely being held together, then you have gone past the point of no return, and it's time for a new pair of shoes.

Wearing shoes for a long time is not necessarily the problem here. It is nice to have a good pair of shoes that will last a long time, and it can save money compared to just throwing them out all the time before they are worn. But if you're worried about whether the shoes will make it through the day or not, then it is time to toss them out.

If you're really dedicated to one pair of shoes, or you find it difficult to find something that fits well, then get a few of the same kind and wear those. No one is really going to notice if you have five of the same pair of shoes and you wear them for a long time.

But they will notice if the shoes start to fall apart, and you keep wearing those old things. Plan and know when it is time to give up on a pair of shoes, even when they are your favorite shoes.

WARDROBE MALFUNCTIONS IGNORED

Wardrobe malfunctions are a part of life. You can't always avoid them. But if you just ignore the malfunctions and allow them to stick around, then it can be embarrassing for your partner to try and cover them up for you.

Men, you want to be prideful about the way you present yourself to the world. Take the time to identify these wardrobe malfunctions and don't ignore them when you go out in public. You are an adult, which means you should be able to put on your clothes the right way and walk out of the house with your clothes matching and no major malfunctions. But for some reason, this ends up causing more issues along the way for men than it does for women.

If there are some holes in your pants, a button missing on your shirt, or some other issue, then get it fixed or choose another outfit. This will help you look more presentable and can save a bunch of eyerolls from your spouse as they try to figure out how to make you change at the last minute.

CHAPTER ELEVEN: GROOMING GOOFS

Men have different grooming needs compared to women. But many men are going to stick with just the bare minimum and do not take care of themselves all that well. It may seem easier, but when you expect your partner to take good care of themselves and look presentable when they go out in public, then you need to do the same for them as well.

There are several grooming goofs that men can make if they are not careful. But you need to learn how to avoid them so that you don't drive your partner up the wall when they see you. Some of the most common grooming goofs that men can make include:

THE UNPREDICTABLE BEARD

The beard is a hassle. Is it going to be long, or short, or somewhere in between? Does your partner need to worry about it scratching them when they come in for a kiss, or will your face be silky smooth sometimes? Not having a predictable beard that you are able to handle can be annoying and will drive the woman in your life crazy.

It isn't that you can never experiment with facial hair occasionally. But when you're changing it all the time, often for no reason, it can start to get annoying. It is much better to consider what looks good on you and stick with it. Try one thing at a time and let it grow on you for a month or more to determine whether you really like it or not. But go for consistency for the long-term.

DROWNING
IN COLOGNE

Your morning is going great, and you are ready to get to work and impress everyone. But then you walk into the kitchen and your spouse's eyes start to water and they begin to cough. This seems like a bit of an exaggeration, and you may wonder what is causing them to act in this manner. In most cases, it is because you are putting on too much cologne and it is overwhelming to the senses.

Many women appreciate when you take the time to put on some cologne; they really do. But there is a limit to how much cologne you can put on and still be acceptable. If it smells like you took a bath in the cologne for an hour or more and anyone who comes near you starts to struggle with breathing, then you probably put on too much for the occasion.

Usually one spritz, maybe two, will be plenty to help you get rid of the bad smells and make them more attractive to the people who are nearby. But it is possible to overdo it, especially when you're around people with sensitive noses or allergies.

Many times, men will choose to use too much cologne to handle bad smells like body odor. If this is the case and you feel like you need a ton of cologne to smell good and not scare everyone away, it is better to take a shower and wash off with body wash and water instead. This can also help you smell good, while making it easier to not drown everyone with the smells either.

It is always best to err on the side of caution with this one. If you are not sure how much of the cologne you should be using, you should use just a little bit rather than a lot. Start out with one spritz and call it quits. The cologne should not be a replacement for a good bath or other hygiene options, and one spritz should be plenty for most people.

Cologne is meant to enhance you and make sure that you can make it through a tough day. But when you don't pay attention to how strong the smell is, or you use it to avoid showering or taking a bath, then everyone is going to notice. Find a cologne that packs less of a punch and only spray a little bit on. If you aren't using enough, your partner will let you know.

IGNORING SKINCARE

While women seem to be fixated on skin care, most men seem to think that a regular bar of soap will be enough to give them the glowing skin they want.

Men, your skincare is important as well, and you need to take some time to focus on it. Washing your face off with some warm water is better than nothing, but when you want to protect your skin, you need to step up to the plate and do a little bit more than that.

The type of skincare products you will need depends on your skin and even the type of work that you do. If you work outside, especially in the winter, you may need a good moisturizer to fight off the elements. Also, don't forget the sunscreen during the summer (this is really something that all men should consider using to protect their skin).

If you have a beard that you shave off, you may need some skin products to avoid some of the razor burn when you are done and to keep the skin fresh and new. For those who suffer from acne and other blemishes, there are some other skincare products that you can use, many of which are formulated for men.

Maybe you aren't sure which skincare products are the best ones for you. Your partner will likely have some good ideas and can at least get you started in the right direction to correct those skin problems.

Coming up with a good skincare routine, even for a guy, can make all the difference. It allows you to get rid of any blemishes, rough patches, and more. When you choose some skin care that has SPF in it, you will be able to protect against the damage possible with the sun too.

TREATING ALL HAIR PRODUCTS THE SAME

Different hair products exist for a reason, so you shouldn't treat them all the same. Some will help with different hair problems, such as dry hair, oily hair, and more. Part of the problem is that many body and skincare products are marketed to work in multiple ways, but this doesn't mean that you should use them that way all the time.

Perhaps you have had this problem in your own home. You have gone down the hair care aisles and just picked out a shampoo or conditioner, not knowing which one your partner often uses. But then it just doesn't work the same way or makes your oily hair worse or your scalp itch because you are drier than usual. You try to get some other hair products and find they don't work the way that you want.

If you plan to use hair products to give your hair some added help, then take the time to find out what they do and then use them properly. This will help you get more out of the product and may save you some money.

You may need to experiment a bit with some of the different hair products that you plan to use. Try a few of them out and see whether you like one more than the other. You can ask a hair stylist for some suggestions if you have no idea where to get started on this, or even ask your spouse to see what they would suggest. This can make it a bit easier for you to pick out the right products for all your needs.

MISMATCHED SHAVING

Shaving is an important part of the male grooming process, and it is important that it is done right. Most men do not shell out for a professional shave every time; this can be time-consuming and expensive since beards may need to be trimmed or shaved once or twice a week, if not daily.

That said, many men struggle with achieving the right shave when they try to do it themselves. Sometimes, it can be hard to see whether the beard

is even when you try to do it yourself. But your partner, and everyone else around you, are going to notice when the two sides of your face don't seem to line up.

There are a few things that you can consider to up your shaving game. If you insist on leaving a little beard, then get the right tools and even look at some tutorials on YouTube or other sites for help managing your beard.

If you've tried everything under the sun and still can't seem to get it all organized and looking amazing, then it may be time to just shave the whole beard off. When you don't leave anything behind, you will find that it is much easier to get both sides to match up and look good when you leave the house.

Shaving is an art form, and you will need to practice seeing what is going to look best on you. Look at some fashion magazines or online to see what is recommended for your type of face or ask your spouse which one they prefer the most. This can give you some place to start on the adventure too. But be sure to practice and be careful as you shave to ensure that you do not end up making a mess of your face.

OVERESTIMATING HAIRCUT FREQUENCIES

Getting a nice haircut can help you look trim and proper, whether you have a more professional job, or your job doesn't care what your hair looks like. When you keep the hair trimmed and neat, it just has a better overall appearance. Knowing how often to get the hair done so that it won't become shaggy and unmanageable can help.

Many men are going to overestimate how often they need to get this hair cut done in the first place. They may have a standing appointment and go in whether the hair needs a trim or not, or they just assume it looks too shaggy and a mess long before it needs to be done. This might feel like great personal time for the man of the house but can end up costing more money and will often leave the spouse at home alone with the children.

Your wife isn't going in all the time to get her hair done, so you don't need to do it either. The actual frequency of when you need to get a haircut will depend on how fast your hair grows and how important keeping it trimmed is to the industry where you work. But there is no point going in and getting another haircut when you can barely tell that the hair has grown at all.

Sure, it is better than letting the hair get overgrown and look bad, but constantly going in for a professional haircut is time consuming and expensive. If you are someone who struggles when the hair grows a little bit, save some money by getting some trimmers to use on your own. This may not be as good as a professional haircut, but it will help you feel better and perhaps you can skip a few appointments throughout the year.

USING ANY AVAILABLE TOWEL

Some families may choose to use a towel more than one time to save on the laundry bill. If you just used a towel to wipe off your face at the end of the day, it can seem silly to throw it in the laundry basket and wash it all over again.

But there does come a time when a towel has been used too often and you need to get it cleaned, rather than using it again and again. Towels do get dirty, and if you are rubbing a dirty towel all over yourself, then it is almost impossible to stay clean even after a shower.

Your spouse likely spends part of her week getting laundry done. While it may seem altruistic that you are saving on towels and using one that is dirty already, there are likely a ton of clean ones that you can rely on as well. Your spouse is not going to feel the love if you try to come up and hug them after using that nasty old towel.

Before you jump into the shower or bath, take a few minutes to go and find your own towel. Find one that is clean and doesn't smell or won't make you feel gross when you are done getting cleaned up. Everyone in the home will thank you.

CHAPTER TWELVE:
FITNESS FUMBLES

Many men will try to start up a new diet or do a workout routine in the hopes of getting in better shape. Whether they want to look better for their partners, have gotten some bad news from their doctors, or they want to be able to keep up with their children better, men will want to see if they can improve their overall health.

While there is nothing wrong with getting healthy and taking care of your body, there are several ways that men will fumble and mess up with their fitness, making it more difficult on the women in their lives. Some of the top "fitness fumbles" that men will make often include:

THE BEER DIET

It is important for everyone to take care of their health. While it may seem like a better option to go out and have fun with your friends, or down a bunch of drinks and unhealthy food on game night, this is going to end up ruining your health.

There is nothing wrong with having a few drinks on occasion to calm down and enjoy life. But when it turns into a diet of its own, this is not a good thing. The beer diet is common with men, and it is expensive and can be harmful to your overall health if you are not careful about it.

To start, the beer diet can be harmful to your health. The alcohol is hard on your liver and all the extra calories that you take in can slow you down and add on the pounds. As your waistline continues to grow and you continue to drink, your health concerns will go through the roof as well.

Another issue is the cost. Alcohol is not cheap, and if you are trying to stay on a budget (or you are making everyone else in the house stay on a budget), then alcohol can take a big chunk out of it. If everyone else needs to pinch their pennies, it can cause a lot of resentment if you keep on drinking every weekend and don't seem to care about the money.

To help keep the finances in order, and to work on being fit, you should consider cutting down on the beer diet and keeping it to a minimum. This doesn't mean that you can never enjoy a drink again, but it does mean that you will not chug down a bunch of beers each night. Keep beer for special occasions and see just how much easier it becomes to reach your fitness goals.

PERPETUAL
DIET STARTING

Men, we applaud you for starting a diet. This is a great way to start eating healthy foods, lose some weight, and keep you around longer. Even though you may drive us crazy, and we want to run away on some days, we do want to keep you around for a long time. But trouble strikes when you're perpetually starting a diet, and then quitting it, just to start up another one again.

First off, it is tiring to hear all about the new diet and all the great benefits. We have plenty of experience with you, and we know how these diets are likely to go when it comes to you. Sure, you have the best of intentions, but we can look at the ten diets you have started and stopped in the past few years, and we know this one has no chance of lasting very long at all. Hearing about how this one is different, and how you are magnificent enough to stick with it (even though it sounds almost impossible or too good to be true) is getting old.

Another issue is that each of these diet plans tend to have specific rules that you need to follow to get the "miracle" results that are promised. Of course, you want to jump right on the bandwagon and give it a try. This means that your partner needs to go out and purchase a whole new meal plan, with plenty of fruits and vegetables and specialty products, just so you can give it a try.

It would be one thing if you stuck with the diet; the food and supplements would get eaten and it wouldn't be a waste. But many times, these items will sit in the fridge and start to wilt away. Then your partner must throw away all that money in the form of food, not to mention how much time it took them to do the shopping in the first place. Don't even mention those supplements that could cost hundreds of dollars and are just cluttering up space.

While there is nothing wrong with going on a new diet and giving it a good try to keep yourself healthy, avoid some of those specialty diets. They may work, but they are hard to commit to and may not work for you. Stick with healthy and wholesome foods, cutting out the sugars, fast food, and beer, and you will see a difference. This will improve your health, while not driving your partner insane.

Do not tell your partner that you are going to start a healthy diet all the time, especially if you are doing something like a juice cleanse, the Keto diet, or another option that requires expensive ingredients. This will just add more work to her plate. Consider just sticking with a diet that is full of healthy fruits and vegetables, dairy, lean meats, fats, and whole grains. This is something that is always in style and can benefit the whole family too.

ABANDONED GYM MEMBERSHIPS

The dreaded gym membership. This is a problem that can be common for anyone, not just men. It is just that men tend to take it to the next level with their promises and overestimate what they can do at the gym. It is admirable that you want to go to the gym and work hard for your health. But when the gym membership costs hundreds of dollars and comes with a contract that is difficult to get out of, we have a problem.

Men, you might spend weeks trying to convince your spouse that a gym membership is going to be great for you. It may be a bit better if it has a childcare option or is a fitness club that is for the whole family, but it can still turn into a big waste if you are not careful. You may have the best of intentions, but then work, kids, and everything else gets in the way, which will make it less likely that you'll be able to see results or even make it to the gym.

If you are going to get a gym membership, then you need to make sure that you will use it. For those who have experience going to the gym before and didn't stick with it, then a regular gym may not be a good option. Looking at some fitness centers with pools, saunas, and classes could be a better option, so everyone in the family is able to use it and get the benefits.

You can also look at whether the gym offers a trial membership for a month or more. This will help you get in for a lower price, or even free. If you are not able to keep with a steady workout routine for at least a week to a month, then it is probably not a good idea to decide to pay for a membership for the whole year right off the bat. See how you do and work from there.

Picking out gyms that allow you to pay month-to-month, and don't have big fees for canceling them if it doesn't work, will be a good idea if you haven't been getting to the gym. You may surprise yourself and go to the gym quite a bit, but you may also wear out after a few days and be unable to keep up. Having some options to see which one holds true for you can save some money, while preventing you from driving your partner insane.

Another option to consider is to just do some of the workouts at home. There are many workouts that you can do using just your own body weight, and you can always take the kids for a nice walk or bike ride to get the heart pumping as well. You can even find workouts online, many of which require minimal equipment. This can make it easier to fit exercise into your busy schedule and will not require as much money when you are first starting out.

MISUSING WORKOUT EQUIPMENT

Maybe you have gotten a gym membership and have dedicated yourself to going to the gym. You have a schedule, and unlike many others, you show up ready to do the work and feel the burn. You should get some credit for that, right?

The issue arises when we look at how you use the equipment in the gym. You can do all the reps you want and add on a ton of weight. But if you are not using the equipment properly, you need to stop and reevaluate. At best, you will not get the results that you want at the gym and feel disappointed in the progress. At worst, you will use the machine in a manner that will hurt you or cause a major injury.

Before you get all excited about going to the gym, you need to learn how to use the equipment correctly. Do not be that annoying gym-goer who is misusing the equipment, the person who takes all the weights so that no one else is able to use them, or the person just sitting on the equipment and doing nothing.

Perhaps you aren't sure how to use the equipment properly, and that makes you a little self-conscious. Don't worry! There are different ways to learn. Many gyms will have diagrams on the equipment that allow you to see the proper way to utilize it. YouTube is also a great resource that will show you how to use each piece of equipment, while giving tips to help you get heavier weights on there.

Another thing to consider is that most gyms will have staff on hand, at least during the daytime hours. If you see a piece of equipment and you are not certain about whether you are using it properly or not, then ask. It is possible to have someone help you with the individual piece of equipment that you would like to use, or you can even get a tour and learn how to use most of the equipment at the same time. This can keep you safe and will help you get the most out of that gym membership you spent so much money on.

Before you decide to purchase some of this equipment to use in your own home, take the time to learn how to properly use it. This will make a difference in how effective the equipment is, while making it easier for you to decide whether that equipment is the right fit. Whether you have weights or a full-body piece of equipment that you want to use, you will find that this can help you really burn those muscles and feel amazing.

EXAGGERATING WORKOUT STORIES

We get it, you had a great workout that got the muscles burning and you feel amazing. Whether you ran a few extra miles, beat a personal speed record, or lifted more weights than ever, you are excited and want to tell the world. Your partner has no problem hearing about some of these workout stories, in the appropriate settings.

The problem occurs when you exaggerate the workout story; woman can usually tell when this is happening. It is one thing to say you got one or two extra reps in than before if you have been working towards that goal. It is another to state that you added 100 pounds of weight overnight or took 5 minutes off your mile in just a week. It just isn't possible, and no one really wants to hear the exaggerated story.

Keep your stories legitimate if you want to get some of the attention you deserve for the work. Know when someone else is interested in hearing about it, and when they are not. Also, be careful who you brag to. You may be able to get away with just an eyeroll when you make up a workout story for your partner. But when you say that same story to someone in the gym, you may be asked to join a competition against them. You will look like the fool when you aren't able to do what you claim.

IGNORING WARM-UPS

No matter your age, it is not a good idea to ignore your warm-ups. You need to pay some attention to a good warm-up, no matter how limited you are on time. The amount of time that you should spend on the warm-up will depend on the type of workout that you plan to do. If you are taking it easy for the day, then a 5-minute warm-up will be fine. If you plan to push it hard, then you may need to spend 10 to 15 minutes warming up before you jump in.

There are a ton of benefits to warming up (and cooling down) before your workout. It helps loosen the muscles and gets the blood flowing, so you are ready to get into the workout. Starting out cold and pushing your body too hard is never a good thing, oftentimes resulting in injuries that can be unpleasant.

Too many guys think they are the exception to the rules and will show up to the gym and jump right into heavy weights or a big run, without doing a warm-up beforehand. Then they get injured, tearing a muscle or causing some other damage. Now all your motivation will go down the drain because you can barely move for a while and may need to spend some time in the hospital recovering.

Rather than having this happen, take the time to do a warm-up. You can ask someone at the gym for advice on doing a good warm-up or look online. It is one of the safest things you can do, especially if you are getting older or you have not done a good workout in a long time. It may slow down your time, but warm-ups can provide you with the safety that your body needs along the way.

If you are uncertain about some of the warm-ups that are available to you, look online. It can depend on the exercise that you would like to get done. For example, if you plan to do an intense walk or jog, then starting with a leisurely pace will help, slowly increasing your pace until you are ready to go. For weightlifting, you can consider using lighter weights or other static stretches, to get started.

CHAPTER THIRTEEN:
FATHERHOOD FLUFFS

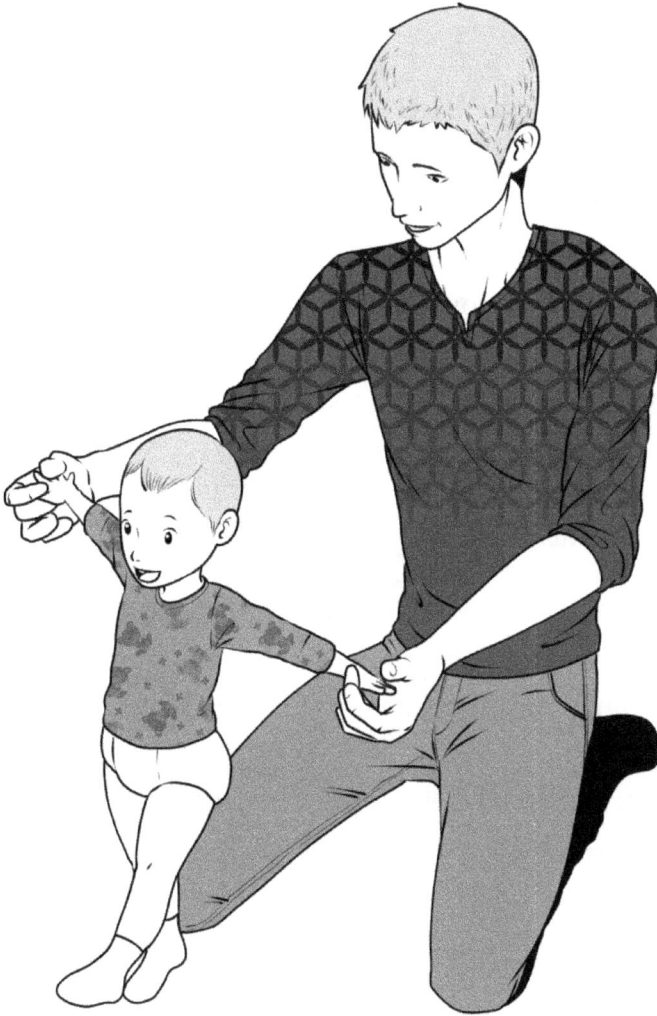

Overall, you are a good dad. You work hard to help support the family, deal with your spouse when is at her wit's end and are a lot of fun with the kids. But there are a few things that dads tend to do that can make parenting harder for mom. Let's take a look at some of the common "fatherhood fluffs" that can happen and some of the simple steps you can take to avoid them and become a better parent to your kids and partner to your spouse.

LATE-NIGHT TICKLE FIGHTS

Your spouse loves that you take the time to play with the kids and have some fun. But do you really need to pick the rowdiest and craziest game to play with them right before it is time to get them settled down to sleep? Sure, the kids aren't going to object, and they will have a ton of fun. But when it is time to get them to sleep, you will be frustrated when the kids are too riled up to go to bed.

It's not that your spouse doesn't want you to spend time with the kids, and there are certainly plenty of occasions when a tickle fight or rough housing is appropriate. But you need to choose your time wisely. For example, if you play these games at 8:25 pm when the kids need to be in bed by 8:30, they will never settle down and you will spend the next hour or more fighting, leaving the kids grumpy the next morning.

There are better activities you can do to help your child get ready for bed and still have some fun with them. Pick ones that are a bit quieter and will not get everyone riled up and ready to go. For example, spend twenty minutes reading. Reading a story with one another can help your kids develop their reading skills and calms them down.

You can even help a bit with the bedtime routine. Help them finish up some of their chores, get ready for a bath, and brush their teeth. You can have some fun with this, without having to turn it into a big war. Don't add more work for everyone when it is bedtime. Pick quiet activities to work on and see how much smoother bedtime can go for everyone.

THE UNIVERSAL "ASK YOUR MOTHER"

Yes, we know. Moms are the all-knowing creatures of the house. They know how often a child needs their medicine when they are sick, where that hidden shoe has gone, and what time to be at the school for that big event. It seems like no matter what question you ask her; she can come up with a response within moments, astounding and impressing everyone who is around.

But do you want to know a little secret? Dads know things as well. They may not be the keeper of the shoes or know the whole schedule, but there are plenty of decisions that they can use their great minds for, without having to put all the burden on mom. When the kids ask about having a dessert or going out with friends, sending them over to mom to get that question answered is not always necessary.

If your child wants to know when their dentist appointment is and you don't know, there are a few steps. Your partner probably has a personal calendar, or a big one in the kitchen, that has all the dates written down. If you aren't sure about when supper is, make an educated guess.

The problem here is that when you don't answer these questions, you shift all the work and responsibility over to your partner. They have already been asked one million questions today, and they really don't need to have more just because dad is too tired to think about it. Mom has had enough of it, so it's time to find a way to answer your child's questions on your own. It's not that she doesn't want to be there to help, but you are an adult and can stand up a bit here. Answering questions is a simple way to do that.

DIAPER DENIAL

Let's just admit it right here and now; no one likes to change a dirty diaper. Babies can make a big mess for such tiny people, and every parent has put it off a bit in the hopes that their partner will step up and be the one to do it this time. Many men opt out of changing diapers at all, putting extra stress and work on mom's shoulders.

When it starts to become obvious that dad hasn't changed a dirty diaper in weeks, and mom is now the one doing it again, you can bet she is noticing and getting angry. She doesn't like changing those diapers any more than you do, but she does understand it needs to get done or the mess becomes worse, and the baby isn't too happy along the way.

Stop being lazy with the diaper changes and help your partner. Preferably, you will take the initiative and be there when the baby has a big blow-out, but helping with any of the diaper changes can make a difference. Keep in mind that your spouse probably catches a lot of them in the evening, and if she is staying home, she gets most of them through the day as well. You can help for those few hours you are at home.

Rather than seeing this as a disgusting chore that you now need to do, see it as some quality bonding time for you and the baby. It may only take a few minutes to clean them up, but you can talk with them, sing some of your favorite songs, or make some fun jokes with them. All of these will help make the work a little less of a chore and the baby will appreciate the time they get to spend with dad. Plus, it can give mom a break and help her feel happy, which makes a big difference in the household too!

PROMISING KIDS WITHOUT FOLLOW-UP

As a dad, you want to promise the kids the world. You want to take them to all the fun stuff, be there every step of the way, and see them smile and be happy with you. This is great. It helps push you a bit farther as a parent and helps you have some goals that will get you to be there for them as much as possible.

The problems occur when you make some promises to the kids, but then never follow-up on them. Whether you never intended to follow up on your promise and just said it to get them off your back, or you just forgot all about it, this is an annoying habit that most men will fall into. Unfortunately, it causes more work for mom and can lead to a good deal of disappointment for the kids.

When you promise the kids something and then don't follow through with it, they aren't going to be happy. However, they aren't likely to approach you about the problem; they are going to go and complain to mom about it. Mom already has enough on her plate and doesn't need to take care of your lack of follow-through. Sometimes, she can't even do anything about it because she doesn't know the specifics of what dad promised. This can be frustrating because she has to explain to the kids why that action won't happen.

In other cases, there may be something the mom can do about the situation, and then she will feel guilt-tripped into doing it because she wants the kids to feel happy. So, she will add more to her plate to get it done, wearing herself out and adding to the frustration.

Don't fall into the lazy habit of promising your kids you will do something with them, and then not following through. It may get them to stop whining to you for a bit, but it doesn't help the situation and makes it look like you can't keep your word. Learn how to stand up to the kids and tell them "no" or find some way to follow through on any action you promise.

OVERESTIMATING MULTI-TASKING WITH KIDS

You used to be a whiz at getting stuff done before you had those kids. You could multi-task and get a big to-do list done during the day. But if you have never tried to get a lot of tasks done with kids around, you will be amazed at how little you will accomplish and how quickly you will be ready to lose your mind during the day.

It is easy to overestimate how much you can accomplish during the day when you are with the kids. Sure, sometimes everyone will get along and no accidents will happen, and they may even step in and help. However, this is not the norm when you have children. In fact, if you ever plan to get this much done when the kids are around, then you will be sorely disappointed along the way.

Always take your to-do list and cut it in half when it comes to estimating what you can get done. This will make everyone a little bit happier when it comes time to get some work done. You will not leave a lot undone that your spouse comes back home to, and you may actually feel like you accomplished something when you can get all of that list done.

Also, do not hand the kids over to your spouse in frustration when you can't get stuff done. She is already working on her own to-do list and doesn't need the kids underfoot. Just because you overestimated your capacity, does not mean she needs to readjust what she has to get done to make it better.

UNDERESTIMATING KIDS' MISCHIEF

It is truly amazing how much mischief young children can get into. When you are not the primary caregiver, it is hard to realize all the trouble that these kids can cause in such a short amount of time.

This can lead to some disasters along the way. The first issue is that the man of the house may not understand why the home is such a mess when they get off work. They assume that since their spouse was there all day to take care of the issues, that the home should be spotless and look amazing. However, if they dare say something, World War III will likely happen.

Kids cause plenty of mischief around the home, and it is hard to slow them down. Your spouse is likely spending a good deal of the day cleaning up, but it only takes a few minutes of going to the bathroom before the home is destroyed again. Between cleaning up, answering a million questions, stopping fights, making meals, and handling all the other work, it is no wonder that she is exhausted by the end of the day. The last thing she wants to hear is about how she didn't get enough done.

In this case, stop judging and get in there and help. Whether you take the kids out for a few minutes to give mom a break, or you help clean up around the home for a few minutes after supper, make it a priority to take care of the issues rather than judging. You were not home all day and didn't have a chance to see what happened. Would you like it if your spouse walked into your work and started judging, without knowing what was going on or even offering to help? Then don't do it to them.

On the other hand, it is possible that the man will not understand the amount of mischief that their kids can make when they take them out on their own. They may make these big plans or assume they can get all their projects done around the home with the kids there, but then total chaos ensues.

Nothing is more annoying than a spouse who is a know-it-all when it comes to the kids. Not only is saying those things enough to make her want to kick you out, but when she comes back to the big mess and half-finished projects at the end of the day, she then has all that extra work to do.

Men, realize that while your spouse may love the kids and spending all that time with them, kids are tough. They can cause plenty of mischief along the way, so don't assume that she isn't doing all she can to take care of them or that she is just being lazy. Plan your day accordingly when you are the one in charge of the kids, and make sure that you step in and help when you get back from work. She deserves it after chasing all those kids.

CONCLUSION

We hope that you were able to get some valuable advice, and a bit of laughter, along the way. There are many blunders that men can make that drive everyone else in the home crazy, but this was meant to provide a humorous look at a list of them all. The woman of the house can probably point out a few that her man has done on occasion. However, now you have this handy guide to help you through the rough times, you can hopefully lessen the chaos around the home.

Whether you are guilty of committing a few of the fumbles in one chapter, or your issues span across a few of them, there is always some room for improvement. Look or ask your spouse to tell you which problems you tend to have the worst time with (don't worry, they have probably told you before and won't be shy about explaining it again), so you can take the right steps to see improvements.

www.ingramcontent.com/pod-product-compliance
Lightning Source LLC
Chambersburg PA
CBHW060238030426
42335CB00014B/1515